Dark to Light

The Memoirs of David Kennedy

Volume One

Copyright © 2021 David Kennedy

Old Meg Publishing

First Serial Rights Reserved by David Kennedy

The right of David Kennedy to be identified as the author of the work has been asserted to him in accordance with the Copyright, Designs and Patents Act 1988.

All rights reserved. No part of this publication may be reproduced, stored in a retrieval system or be transmitted, in any form or by any means without the written permission of the author.

ISBN certified - 9798499405611

Old Meg Publishing (OMP™)

Available in paperback and on Amazon Kindle

www.facebook.com/oldmegpublishing
www.oldmegpublishing.com

Daniel K Kennedy – (**OMP™**) Founder

The Illustrations on the cover are licensed and copyrighted by David Kennedy

Foreword

For anyone that has known me, briefly or for many years, I hope this explains a little why I am the way I am.
I'm sure most people I've encountered think I've acted strangely on at least one occasion.

For anyone who is affected by the issues covered in this book, I hope you can overcome them and that my story can give support to a handful at least.

There are some helpful contacts and references at the end.

Contents

			Pg
Introduction			3

Volume One

Chapter One	-	1976 to 1986	11
Chapter Two	-	1986 to 1989	23
Chapter Three	-	1989 to 1992	47
Chapter Four	-	1994 to 1997	77
Chapter Five	-	1997 to 2003	87
Chapter Six	-	2003 to 2007	91
Chapter Seven	-	2007 to 2011	99
Chapter Eight	-	2011 to 2013	117
Chapter Nine	-	2013 to 2014	125
Chapter Ten	-	2014 to 2015	131
Chapter Eleven	-	2015 to 2016	139
Chapter Twelve	-	2016 to 2019	145
Chapter Thirteen	-	2019 to 2020	149
Chapter Fourteen	-	2020 to 2021	159

Volume Two

494 Sunsets Remaining	-	December 2020	179
493 Sunsets Remaining	-	January 2021	181
492 Sunsets Remaining	-	February 2021	183
491 Sunsets Remaining	-	March 2021	185
490 Sunsets Remaining	-	April 2021	187

Introduction

I've attempted to "write" a number of times over the past few years, either through blogs or starting to sketch out ideas for a book, before scrapping each one soon after.
I've heard the line "Everyone has one good book in them" somewhere in the past, a sentiment I tend to agree with and I'd think about it every few months, before making another attempt.
Two things would stop me…..over-analysis and lack of self-belief, neither of which I've managed to overcome, but it's time for another go and this time I think I can go through with it.

Over-analysing is a strange trait, with pros and cons that seem to weigh quite close to 50/50. On the one hand there are clear benefits to researching, or at least checking something out online before doing it. But if you spend more time analysing than doing, it starts to become an issue. I have already (156 words in) stopped to look up 3 points and wasted more effort clarifying things than actually putting anything "on paper".
The first thing I researched was also a great example of the dichotomy of over-analysing, as I wondered where the "one good book" quote came from. I discovered that it's attributed to Christopher Hitchens but as a longer quote that I don't believe I'd heard before.

"Everyone has a book in them and that, in most cases, is where it should stay"

Over-analysis AND questioning self-belief all in one quote, nice work!
Clearly, I was right to research the quote as it's a lot more interesting than my throwaway attempt at self motivation. On the other, it exacerbates my fears of spending time creating something that nobody may be interested in.

https://interestingliterature.com/2015/04/who-said-everyone-has-a-book-in-them/
Despite this, I'm definitely going to continue to over-analyse, but will plough on regardless, just leaving the issue of self-belief. This has been my main stumbling point in all previous attempts, with my eventual conclusion being that, whether anyone reads it or not, I want (and need) to do this for myself as a cathartic exercise.
Even after coming to this decision, my writing efforts still fizzled out each time, due to changes in personal circumstances which will come to light in the book. This time is different though, I'm sure of it!

So about this book then. Along with explaining the convoluted background to the meaning of the title, I want to use this introduction to clarify the overarching concept I have in mind.

It won't be fully completed until January 2062, or I'm no longer here to finish it. I see it as a "living book", with Volume One being a sort of a life story / autobiography, cataloging the events of my life from birth through until April 2021.

I will continue to update the online version, Volume Two at least once in each of the following months until January 2062.

I feel that after a difficult first half of my life, I'm at a clear turning point where everything could begin to fall into place. I believe that someone who enjoys reading Volume One of this book would be interested in following the story as it unfolds in real time. And just writing about things helps my mental health anyway.

In previous failed efforts I have struggled to find a comfortable writing style and this has been a contributing factor to a couple of the short-lived attempts. I consider myself to be fairly literate, I like to be grammatically correct and am pretty much 90% confident with spelling. However I don't have a clue how to actually "write". I'm sure there are several key do's and don'ts to create "proper" writing, but that's not something I've been taught at any stage, although I still managed to achieve a GCSE C in both English Language and Literature without really trying.

So I'm going to just write it how I want to, which may be a little unorthodox. In style and content. I have included links to music videos at important points, which I hope you'll watch to see the relevance of the lyrics or overall message. Music has played a massive part in my life and sometimes I think it's easy to listen to songs without actually Listening. My friend Mark is a notable extoller of this virtue!

Another major factor when I've given up writing before is that I'd tried to dress it up as a book about one thing, while having to insert my back story as a side note. In reality I now see that I want to write about what I've experienced in my life, but up to now haven't had the self belief to approach it in such a direct manner. After all, why would anyone be interested in what I have to say?

So how did the title come about? For a long time I used the working title - 500 Sunsets Remaining. Although I've now realised that moniker is more suitable for Volume Two.
This earlier title came about as, in 2020 I embarked on a new routine of getting up to watch the sunrise on the 1st of every month. I guess the title should have been - "500 Sunrises Remaining" but that doesn't quite trip off the tongue and "Sunset" is a more appropriate metaphor in this context.
I began performing this monthly pilgrimage after taking part in a National Trust event called Dawns Live on 16th May 2020 - https://dawns.live/
The premise was for people all over the UK to get up before dawn and either go for a walk or sit somewhere to watch the transition from night through to sunrise. There was a website where you could listen to a

broadcast that began with the Narrator, based in John o' Groats, the first location on the mainland that would see the sunrise.

As this line moved Westward across the country, musicians joined one by one until there was a quintet which included a harp, flute, and piano, playing a specially commissioned piece of music.

It was well executed and did feel like a communal event, so I wondered if people would take part in something like this on a regular basis.

My plan was to find a nice place to watch the sunrise on the 1st of each month, preferably in different locations. One of my rituals is to have a list of all important dates in the coming month and spend some time thinking about those. Mainly birthdays and deathdays (as I call them) along with other anniversaries, notable calendar dates and planned events to look forward to.

I partly did this as my memory is so patchy that I often miss important dates and have little grasp on the passage of time, such as how many years ago people died.

I started a blog around this new "religion" and even tried, via social media, to get a few people to join me to try to recreate the communal aspect (to no avail).

On the 1st of June 2020, while I sat watching the sun rise at 510am near the Crook o'Lune, I wondered how many times I'd do this, if I kept it up monthly for the rest of my life…...say I live to 80, that's, what, 35 years…..times 12 is 420 months. Four hundred and twenty.

It struck me as both a large number and a small number at the exact same time.

I thought this concept would be a good idea for a blog, but the short form style didn't really leave a way for me to weave in my convoluted back story. I need long form, as evidenced by this Intro alone, never mind the anticipated completion date of January 2062. That date was eventually picked as I simply rounded the months up to 500 for aesthetic value, arbitrarily giving myself about another 40 years to live!

So to come back to the explanation of the title, when I decided to add Volume Two to my idea, it made sense to give this the name "500 Sunsets Remaining" as chronologically that's (sort of) where it begins.
On the flip side, I have been calling my monthly blogs "Dark to Light", but that has actually turned out to be the perfect name for Volume One, on a number of levels.

And so concludes the Introduction, now comes the hard part....

Volume One

Chapter One

1976 to 1986
Age 0 to 10

My memories of early childhood are sketchy, generally speaking, with a few stand out events being the only clear recollection I can manage.
I can be forgiven for not remembering the first very short chapter of my life, being born in Dulwich, South London and moving to Hertford when I was around 6 weeks old.

But what I can recall from the next ten years is patchy at best. I'm not sure why this may be, I mean, I was knocked off my BMX bike by a car when I was about 8, but escaped practically untouched apart from a few minor battle scars. So I can't see it being that.
I was the youngest of 3 boys, all pretty much one year apart and despite being similar ages I never quite seemed to be on the same wavelength as Carl and Adam. They were very alike in a lot of ways, although one main difference was their temperament. Both were very mischievous, getting into minor scrapes and occasional fights. Adam seemed more cheeky and roguish, while Carl was moody and rebellious.
I, on the other hand, have always been more sensible, less likely to break the rules and quite shy and quiet, but not to any detriment in my life up to 10 years old.

In hindsight I think that the genes from my mum's side of the family are more prominent in *my* characteristics, while my brothers take after my dad and grandads traits.
Another indicator of this is that I have a small birthmark on my right ear that my mum's dad also had, but no one else in the family, as far as I know.

I'm thinking hard to picture my earliest memories, so I can put these thoughts into a loosely chronological order. This has started to uncover many events I had "forgotten" which I will start to remember as a side effect of writing about it.
I knew this would be a good cathartic exercise.

There are also names of friends and other kids at school that are beginning to pop into my head as I trawl through this foggy sea of memories hoping to bring more details to the surface.
As a part of the process of writing this book, I'd be interested to get in touch with some of these old acquaintances, reporting any new information in Volume Two.
There are people whose real names I won't use, which will be made clear at the time.

So, the first clearly dated memory I can muster is when we were getting ready to leave the house heading for the cinema to see E.T, which I knew was a surprise for Carl's birthday.

This must have been around January 1983, so I would be 6 years old.

It was a rare treat for us to see a film at the cinema and I remember putting my coat on and excitedly saying "ET phone hooome" without realising that Carl was standing behind me. I don't know if he heard me, or if that gave the surprise away, even to this day.

I'm not sure I've ever spoken to him about the incident. I don't recall much else about the day, either specifically watching the film or if we went for a meal or whatever.

I'm sure there are some events buried in my memory banks before this, but not with enough detail to be sure of ages, or what parts I've fabricated to fill in the blank spots.

Is it strange that I can't remember anything before the age of 6? Plenty of other people have a similar level of recollection I'm sure, but my wife, Taylor (not her real name) has clear memories of events as young as 3.

The vague picture I can paint before age 6 would be Christmas mornings or maybe visiting relatives, but any specifics or dates are hard for me to pin down.

One constant in my early life was that I always had Spectrum computers, from the early rubber keyboard 48k machine, through to the 128k+, with built in "Datacorder", don't you know!

The 1983 release date of the 48k Spectrum would put me around 7 years old, which seems right, maybe getting one when I was about 8?
I do have a faint recollection of unwrapping the 128k version, which was a joint Christmas present a few years later.

https://www.tomshardware.com/uk/reviews/history-of-computers,4518-26.html

It's crazy to think that the Playstation 5 is now 64 bit, and they stopped improving this element of the processing power with the PS2 in 1990. I don't understand the size difference from 48k in Bytes, to a next generation consoles 64 Bits, but I know the speed of progress is dramatic. It follows Moores Law with almost scary accuracy.

https://en.wikipedia.org/wiki/Moore's_law

So I do remember spending hours playing games and even attempting to write basic programs, starting with the help of a magazine where you just copied the code word for word.
But mainly playing games…….like probably 98% games.
One clear memory I have is during the summer holiday when I was about 9, I would rather sit playing Daley Thompsons Decathlon than go outside and do some actual running around.

To the point where my mum told me I had to go out and get some sun, so I set up a little area just out of the back door and pulled the computer and monitor outside and carried on button bashing!

Some of the games were amazing for their time and will always be iconic for me.
The playability and high level of challenge made them much more entertaining than some of the overly produced "blockbusters" of today.
And these regular £1.99 bargains came from the likes of Codemasters, or the occasional glossy looking game by Ocean for £9.99. These usually had a big fancy box cover and maybe a poster included, to warrant the higher price tag.
These early, rough around the edges, knockabout games paved the way for the incredible leap forward in technology that in the space of a few years has generated epic worlds like Final Fantasy and Red Dead Redemption, as just two off the cuff examples.
There are great games around now, more than I have time to play properly. But the current high cost of a single game puts a bigger expectation on the experience, which more often than not ends in disappointment in some aspects. I think the controls have become too complex and playability has been lost. I'd love to see a return to more straightforward fun games, one good current example of which is Streets of Rage 4.

Another dateable fact is that we definitely had a few early editions of Crash! Magazine, which was first published in February 1984.

https://archive.org/details/crash-magazine?&sort=-date&page=3

It's great looking through this archive and still recognising some of the cover art and the Tips & Cheats page. No way my brain would find that information by itself, so such clear pictorial evidence is really helpful to me.

I also collected Quest magazine, which I presume my mum bought for me every fortnight.
I don't think I completed the 60 issue set, but I definitely had a good number of them, including the special 20th Anniversary of the Apollo mission edition - Space: The Final Frontier

http://www.partworks.co.uk/contents/en-uk/d141.html

Individual issues can be found for sale on eBay and the archive above is interesting to look through, if only to see the reason I wasn't able to build the sundial or many of the other projects! Maybe with a little more help or interest from my parents in this area, I would have achieved more. Not that this particularly made them bad parents, just hamstrung by the pressures of daily life with 3 kind of annoying boys causing chaos.

Another relatively lucid recollection I have is that our next door neighbour's cat had kittens, one of which I picked to keep and called Tiffy. Our nans dog was called Taffy, which I liked and as our cat was female I tweaked it to Tiffy.
I have a great photo of me holding her in the back garden, which I'll dig out to see if it helps uncover any further details.

Overall I'd have to say my life was pretty ordinary, at least up until we moved house when I was starting my final year in Primary School.

Being uprooted can sometimes be an unavoidable event and to be honest the timing wasn't the worst for me in a lot of ways. I hadn't made any particularly close friends during this period, either at school, or around our estate. Not that I was a loner, but most of my time would be spent at home or with my brothers when playing outside. I did have one friend, but can only remember small snippets of irregular meetings. Just across from the corner of our terrace of houses, Richard Hackett lived with I assume his mum and dad. I barely recall his dad, but the house was uniquely decorated inside, with the living room having a parody Bayeux Tapestry all around the walls. In the toilet that was downstairs, the entire walls were covered with comic book style clippings, that I didn't really understand, but could tell were funny. I may be misimagining the scale, but I'd love to see it again to confirm if I remember one particular detail. The last panel of one comic strip was in an office, where the (I assume) Secretary was caught in a suggestive pose with the boss commenting " 'kin 'ell" in a speech bubble.
My naive mind wondered if that was a nickname or some play on words that I didn't get. I guess the colloquial abbreviation at least did the job of making the humour work for adults and not kids, where "fuckin hell" would have kind of spoiled the joke. I

assume these random pieces of artwork were by his dad and he was an artist of some kind. I love seeing graffiti in some instances now, especially bad toilet graffiti. I blame this interest on you Mr Hackett!

I don't remember much of Richard himself either, or even if I called him Rich, or some other nickname. No idea if he called me by my first name, or a nickname. Names are quite a big ordeal for me for some reason. I have a weird anxiety about using anyone's name out loud, even feeling odd saying my wife's name in some situations.
I know that's strange, or at least I think I'm in a minority with this one. But there are reasons for it that will come to light I'm sure.
The one event I can describe is when Richards Labrador had puppies, I had called around to see him for something unrelated, but my main memory of the encounter was the dog being aggressive to protect her pups. For some reason I feel this led to me not going inside the house, or maybe I never went round again after that. The timeline around that is very unclear, so I could be wrong about the details, but the "highlights" of the events are mainly solid.

That's it I think, for friends in an estate teeming with kids around my age.
I can't say I even had a best friend at either of the primary schools that I went to. Again, the dates are a mystery, but I know I went to a school actually on the

estate for at least one year. Can't say I know the names of any teachers, or students though. (sorry guys if anyone remembers me fondly!)
The next school I do remember, called Wheatcroft, which was at the bottom of "Gallows Hill". There was a big conker tree next to the school fences, which created plenty of entertainment for a few weeks every year. I'm struggling to bring back the names of anyone I knew there, Daniel Marshall? I'm sure Daniel Marshall was the lad who broke his leg in the last year I was there. He was one of the best footballers so this was big news, for an already popular kid.

There was also a girl I liked called Nia (99% sure that's right) from Wales.
Do I remember sitting behind her in assembly, fascinated by her crimped hair and not really knowing why? I'm sure that happened. I would have been too young to know how to talk to her, but it was soon after that when we moved away to the North West, so any friendship was soon snuffed out.

Outside of school, I can't remember any names or many other kids in a positive light from our estate. The three main incidents all involved me getting moderately injured, good going for someone that aims to avoid trouble.
The location, date and back story are lost to me, but a kid that didn't like Carl or Adam recognised me as their brother and threw a rock at me from across the

road, hitting me on the head. I had to sit with a warm flannel on my head for ages trying to get all the blood out of my hair after that one.

Another kid, just metres from our house, threw a stick at me which had sharp thorns that dug into my head, with less serious damage than the rock.

The third and worst event must have been when I was around 8.

I was chasing Carl on my bike and followed him down an alleyway, I didn't see him bear left into a car park and I rode straight in front of a car that was luckily driving at a slow speed.

After spending only one night in hospital, I was back home and my next hazy memory related to this event was a policewoman asking me what speed I thought the lady was driving. I felt slightly pressured to say she was driving too fast, to take the focus off me. But I knew it was my fault and in normal circumstances I would be quite safe crossing roads or even playing in the street.

I don't remember talking about it again so I assume it was resolved amicably.

When we lived in Hertford my parents rarely went out for meals or for drinks, but one of their friends owned a pub about half an hour drive away, so they would occasionally visit them for a night out.

Most of the time we would all go, as there was a nice beer garden with a kids play area.

My dad would have a few pints and still drive home after, I wouldn't know how much or if it was really just one or two, but I definitely had the impression that he shouldn't have been driving.

Nothing bad ever happened but it has stuck in my mind for some reason.

Once we were back home it seemed to be standard practice that they would have an argument over some petty disagreement. I hated hearing it while I was trying to go to sleep, it gave me a horrible sense of fear that I didn't understand. I blocked out as much sound as possible but I could still hear them so I kept repeating "stop arguing" over and over to myself to drown them out. Luckily this wasn't a regular occurrence as it really did upset me. I think since that point I always knew that my parents weren't happy together, almost like they just stayed married "for the kids". I'll never understand that approach as I would rather be in a happy one parent household than a miserable family unit.

My brothers had already gained a little bit of a reputation as troublemakers at the primary school and around the estate, which was another benefit to relocating. Not that it was anything that serious, but I know I have been judged by people just by association of my name and not in a positive light.

At the age of 12 and 13 Carl and Adam were setting fire to stuff and smoking in the bushes.

I don't think I tried smoking until I was in my 30's

Chapter Two

1986 to 1989
Age 10 to 13

So a fresh start in a new town, beginning with the final year of Primary School, a good chance to get settled in before the jump to High School. In this respect, I feel my brothers had a harder situation to deal with, going into a strange place as your first or second year in Secondary School. Their more boisterous characters were better suited to this than mine though, and I had a year to make some friends that might go to the same high school as me.

My general understanding of the situation is that my parents had slipped into a fair amount of debt, nothing out of the ordinary but quite wisely made changes to fix the problem.
Our house was worth about £70,000 and my dad had the chance to move jobs to a company in Liverpool. Due to the North/South divide, property was a lot cheaper so I believe they managed to remortgage to clear all debts and buy a house for about £40,000. This all makes sense to me, but doesn't take into account personal factors, like being able to visit family relatively easily, leaving out the mild damage to my non-existent circle of friends.
 Although for me, the main damage to the strength of my extended family relationships had already been

done when we originally left London. Most of our tribe were from around the West London area, with some having moved slightly further out but within easy reach.
Our move left us in close-ish proximity to Grandparents and Aunties and Uncles, but not easily accessible.
We saw them all semi-regularly but I think it would have been nice to live in the same area as one of them, allowing us to grow up together as a close extended family unit.

This pattern seemed to work its way through our family tree, with uncles, aunties and cousins leaping to new locations, South Wales, Oxford, Cornwall, even Ireland. This stretching of our family bonds has made it hard to have meaningful relationships with extended family.

I'm not 100% sure of when we moved, but think I started the September 1986 term at my new Primary school in the 4th and final year, so just before then.
I don't specifically recall a moving day, or many of the events surrounding it like going into our new house for the first time. There aren't any tearful goodbyes I can picture involving people from school or the estate. Overall quite a non-disruptive relocation, with a chance to start afresh, although it's not like I was aware of these points at the time. I just did what I did and tried to do well at school.

Adam had a pony that also had to be transported to a stables close to our new house, which was quite a palaver and I'm sure not long after the move he started to be more interested in the girls at the stables than the horses. He still rode and liked to compete in some show jumping and cross country events, but somewhere over the next couple of years he grew out of it and the pony was sold.
I was always jealous that I wasn't able to have a pony, or had the chance to ride Rascal more myself. I think I would have been pretty decent and after riding quite a lot a few years later, consider myself to be an able, if out of practice rider.

The main issue that sticks in my mind from the initial days in my new school, was my concern over the differences in accent, which were quite extreme in some ways. I learnt very quickly that saying "claarss" instead of "classs" for example, would end in ridicule for sounding like a little posh git. So I changed all my "aarsses" to "assses" and a few other tweaks almost immediately, but as I didn't particularly like the scouse sounding accent, I kept a southern sounding rhythm, with northern pronunciations. It's strange not to have a distinguishable accent, which over time has turned into a sort of yorkshire twang with cockney sprinkles. In doing this I think I avoided any bullying as I didn't really draw attention to myself. Carl took a different approach, starting slowly, but launching full on into a fake scouse after a while, with authentic phlegmy bit at the end of some words if you were lucky.

I was shown around my new school by a lad called Jamie, I can't remember the surname but I'm sure his dad owned the model village on Southport Promenade. I've tried to look it up online, but I think I'd have to go to wherever Newspaper microfiche are kept these days to find more information.
He was nice enough and I went round to his house at least once, with the ever confusing issue of what "dinner" and "tea" mean in different areas. When I heard what they were having for their dinner, which was something like beans on toast or another snack, I was confused and said what I was having, until we figured out that to them dinner is lunch, and tea is an evening meal. Whereas I was taught that the afternoon meal is called lunch and tea is a drink, with dinner being the evening meal.
These minor language barriers were easily broken down, although it did leave me lacking a bit of confidence when meeting new people. But a year to acclimatise, paving the way for another new start, where I would know a few people and find it easier to make friends in High School.

Now that I've begun putting these previously scattered thoughts down in black and white, several names and events have started to come back to me and I can flesh these out with details I'd otherwise inadvertently buried.

Some of the names that spring to mind from 4th year of Primary School -

- Jamie
- Sean
- Jackie Instone
- Louise Leather (Crapnell)
- Emmaleen
- Lindsay
- Kin Wai Chau
- Gareth Withers
- Michael Payne
- Tony Ellington

Despite being "buddied up" with Jamie, I don't think we ever became real friends although I don't know why. The main friend I made early on was Sean. I wish I could remember his surname and I can't believe it's not come to me yet. He lived around the corner, just off the main road that we were on, so only one block away. We got on really well and liked a lot of the same things. If events transpired differently I'm positive we would have turned into lifelong best friends in time.

He too appeared to have moved up from down south, although I still can't geographically place his accent with any accuracy. He no doubt told me where they were from but it's a blank to me.

His more exuberant ways allowed him to keep his accent and front it out, but I was relatively comfortable with my decision to compromise. He definitely sounded cooler than me anyway, with possibly a thick Essex twang, which is my best guess at where they came from.

His parents were Penny and Gary, although I'm not sure Gary was his real dad. Either way, they seemed to break up and get together again every so often. I have some foggy story in my head that Sean's dad (Gary or some other dude) was a work rider for Ginger McCain, and rode the three time Grand National winner Red Rum in training on the beach.........

Ellison!

That's it I'm certain, the name Billy Ellison came to mind, yep a quick web search and found a great article from 2013 where he talks about it.

https://www.liverpoolecho.co.uk/sport/other-sport/horse-racing/riding-red-rum-like-driving-3010812

That would also tie in with the region, as the home of racing in Newmarket borders the County of Essex.
So Sean Ellison it must have been. And Gary wasn't his dad. But he was the father of Ricky (about 7 at the time?) and a little girl younger than that whose name escapes me.

Off on a bit of a tangent now, (according to the writing tips I've read, something you should never do!) as there is one condition I suffer with that I know has affected my life dramatically, of which I remember a perfect example in Sean's house one morning.
I would have walked up to his house so we could go across to school together, which was literally just over the main road.
He was finishing his breakfast, which was a bowl of cereal. As was often the case, he was running late and was eating as quickly as possible.
Sat across the table from him, I had an instant, involuntary and extreme reaction as he slurped the milk and the rushed actions caused his teeth to click on the spoon.

It's hard to explain the sensation, but it's like intense panic.
I honestly didn't know whether to scream or run out of the room.
I can't remember exactly what I did at the time, but I'd think Sean would have noticed I was acting oddly.

I had no idea that this was an actual condition at the time, but in recent years I have discovered a whole community of people with the same issue.
It's called Misophonia. One short description explains –

"Misophonia sufferers have an adverse reaction to certain noises or sounds. Typically these sounds include chewing, lip smacking, tapping, crunching, rustling and other common day-to-day sounds."

The easiest way I can suggest to understand it is to read through the Allergic to Sound website, it's probably the best source of info I've found all in one place.

https://allergictosound.com/what-is-misophonia/

There are also various social media support groups that I have found helpful.

However, officially, it is still yet to be considered a diagnosable condition.
The officials are wrong!

https://en.wikipedia.org/wiki/Misophonia

My description would be that it's like a tourettes tick that occurs when you hear certain noises. You really can't control your reaction and it's definitely a fight or flight instinct.

And it isn't an issue that the person making the noise should be concerned about, it is the condition that affects the sufferer that is to blame for any negative reactions.

Figures I've seen suggest a possible prevalence of about 20%, so potentially one in five people has some degree of Misophonia to "silently" deal with.

There are even separate social media support groups for people who simply *live* with someone who has Misophonia, which I think is great as it can't be easy to deal with on an ongoing basis.

I've recently discovered a bonus, related condition called Misokinesia, which can cause a similar adverse reaction when a repeated movement is made. For example twiddling with hair, bouncing a foot up and down or other repetitive fidgety movements.

I do have a mild sensation with some motions, although it's nowhere near as intense as with sounds. It's more like the side of my face is being gently sandpapered all the time it's happening. I find if I turn my head so the fiddling is out of my eye line, I can forget about it.

This is a bit of a divergence from the story, but it's something that has seriously affected me throughout my life and that I still have to deal with on a daily basis.

Standard practice is to create situations that negate the effect as much as possible, like making sure the TV is on or some music around meal times. Other than that, it is a minor glitch that I can cope with reasonably well most of the time.

Overall, the best way I've found to approach it is to pay it as little attention as possible. So I feel it's best to address it fully now, and other than a couple of specific examples, pretty much ignore it and get on with other threads of the story.

Safe to say, if anyone reads this and has Misophonia, or even found out about it here, then I'd love to hear from you to understand how you have tried to live your life with it.
You have my utmost sympathy regardless, along with anyone close to you that's had to endure this cruel condition.

I'm not sure how my Misophonia came about, it's not known what triggers it initially, or whether it's hereditary. The earliest examples I can recall were at about 11 years old, being deliberately late to sit down for dinner (evening meal) in the hope the rest of the family had eaten a fair bit of their food.
Then I would hold out for as long as I could, before saying I needed the toilet, giving me a good chance all were finished by the time I was back. This routine couldn't be used every day obviously, but it helped me through some tough times!
I now believe my mum also suffers with Misophonia, as she used to tut and huff when my dad was eating.

Understandably so, as he did chomp like a horse in a bucket of oats!

She also used to make her own noise, seemingly in retaliation for every time my dad made a particularly loud munch.

Mum did this weird clicking thing in her throat as she ate, but if that was a way for her to cope with her Misophonia, it only exacerbated mine. You would think she would have noticed my odd behaviour at meal times and see that it was similar to her frustrations. A simple private chat about it at the time could have helped us both and given us a closer relationship.

Following the breakfast incident, I'm not sure if my strange behaviour in a normal situation was a factor, or if Sean even noticed there was any problem, but I don't feel we ever got to be really close best friends, although he was something close to that.

We will come back to Sean later on, but looking at the others on the list the name Lindsay is in the next vault of my memory bank.

She lived directly across the road from us and I think went to the same year in Primary School.

I imagine I had a minor crush on her but was still slightly too immature to understand these feelings. She was sort of tomboyish and the brief interactions we had were pleasant and not too uncomfortable. But we moved on to different schools and another potentially normal route to the early teenage rites of passage was scuppered.

There are flashes of memories of my final day in Primary School, where we were allowed to sign each other's shirts and ties and generally cause chaos.

I've still got those along with my report cards from Secondary School.

Those make enlightening reading for sure.

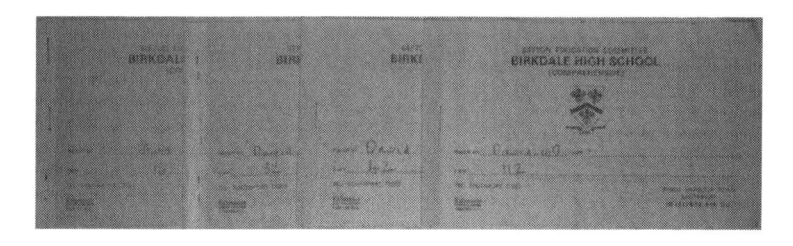

I was childishly excited when my tie was signed by both Louise Leather and Jackie Instone, as to me they were the two of the best looking and more fun girls in our year.

Emmaleen was also very nice and easy to talk to, if a little quiet and standoffish from what I remember.

Kin Wai Chau was a ridiculously intelligent Chinese lad, who was also in some of my classes at High School.
I really liked him, he seemed friendly and interesting, but I never actually made friends with him.
There are other names scribbled on my shirt that I recognise, although I can't picture faces in any detail.

But other than Sean, no other real alliances made with anyone there, or otherwise locally, to take forward into the unknowns of "big school".

Another major decision in my life, that I had no part of, was *which* high school to choose, in this unfamiliar town. I think due to my brothers volatile record up to then, the option taken was for an all boys school. There was an associated all girls school in the area about a mile away.
The other school in the area was a Catholic 6th Form, who were supposedly the mortal enemies of the all boys. I never understood these mini tribal rivalries, I'd rather avoid confrontation.

So the switch to an all boys school distanced me further from what I would call a normal life.
My personal view is that it's not healthy to have separate sex schools as it's not teaching real life situations. Regardless of the difficulties in controlling groups of rowdy teenagers, the challenges are worth the more likely upbringing of a well rounded character.
I think if it wasn't for my brother's reputation, I would have gone to a more "ordinary" school and lived a completely different life by now.

Into this softcore version of borstal I went, with a name already slightly tarnished by my older brothers, but in turn possibly offering at least some protection from bullies in my first weeks.

I feel like I had a reasonably straightforward start in my first year, doing well in all the subjects I liked, and ok in the others. It was obvious to me even at a young age that a teacher can make all the difference when dealing with one specific subject. I loved anything to do with science, but our old, disinterested, sometimes clearly drunk, Biology teacher destroyed any chance I had of doing well or enjoying this branch. Mr Wright in contrast made "Double-Chem" as he mockingly called it, seem like time spent mainly having fun and less like learning, while actually absorbing a lot of information.

And on a personal front, there were enough distractions and other kids more bulliable than me to see me through without any trouble. It's not that I was greatly concerned by the thoughts of other kids picking on me, but I seemed to know that if you started on the wrong foot, you could become an easy target, which would make school a long five year stretch.

So my plan, albeit mostly subconsciously, was to not draw attention to myself and get along with a few people while trying to build a little group of friends. The helpful distractions started in the first week as one lad was late joining by a few days after falling off something and twisting his groin. Everyone knew his name, yet not what he looked like. With the usual childish exaggerations twisting the latest version of this story so that he had jumped off a roof, landed on his balls atop a post and had to have one removed! I don't actually remember what he was called, so it must have got him a rubbish nickname.

There was another Dave in our year, he also moved from "dahn sarf" to up north, but made the crucial error that I had avoided, by not adjusting his accent. Every time I saw him some older lads would be mildly bullying him and mimicking his every word with extra cockney twang for effect. Nothing major but much better to dodge the initial problem in the way I had.

I'm not sure how long it was before my High School "plan" went off track, this is the period of my life where recollection of events is thinnest. Although as I've seen with my earlier years, more "new" memories filter through, or vague incidents gather more detail, when I start to write about it from the perspective that I am now.

I am reading through my report cards to help jostle free some long forgotten nuggets of information. I've got all of them except for the 2nd year, which is a shame.

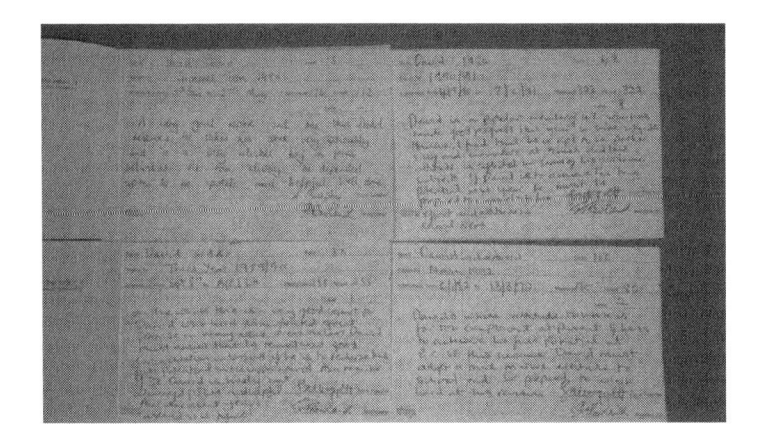

I come across as a model student, polite and helpful with high grades. At least in the earlier examples of these mini time capsules.

Some elements of the teachers' appearances come back to me as I see their names again, starting with the Headmaster, Mr Rowland. It shows the underestimated power of a well struck nickname that my first thought was "Noodle-Heeaad!!" upon seeing his signature. He seemed like a nice enough guy, but tight black curly hair was enough to damn him to be eternally known as noodle head by year after year of annoying kids.

Mr Rimmer. Say no more, other than at the time we didn't know the potentially hilarious meaning to the name our French teacher had. Our year was the first after the cane had been abolished, but Mr Rimmer kept his willow stick and could enforce discipline just as strongly by slamming this cane down on the desk and bellowing SILEEENCE!

He was a good teacher.
One stand out incident in his class was when a new kid called Piers joined mid-term, coming from a private school for some reason. To me he came across as being a year older and much tougher than most of our class. I went for the avoidance tactic and never really interacted with him.
What took place in the build up to this disturbance I can't recall, but it ended with Mr Rimmer picking Piers up by the shoulders and shaking him like a rag doll. The nerdier corner of the classroom I was sat in came up with the convoluted nickname "Piers Lough, Anglo Saxon hamster, shaken, not stirred". You see his name is Piers, he's got big front teeth, and he's just been shook by Rimmer. Not the best effort I know, but memorable at least.

Mr Rigby is a teacher I have only one memory of, that is when I had bad hay fever and he singled me out in front of the class to ask if I'd been sniffing glue, citing my brothers as an example. I definitely didn't get upset but it did have a crushing effect on me, to be publicly accused of basically taking drugs when I'd always just been a good kid.
My classmates would likely think I was upset anyway, when it was really hay fever.
From then on I began to question what the rest of my teachers thought of me, which isn't healthy. Even in my worst report card, I am quite well behaved and get at least a mildly positive review.

Outside of school, one event that can't escape me is when I found my cat Tiffy dead next to the curb, as I was crossing the road to get the bus to school. I know the date as it was the morning after Bonfire Night, so November the 6th, but what year? Must have been during my first year. 1988 when I was 12. It is the only time I know where I took the day off without actually being ill.

I felt a bit embarrassed about it going in the next day and this didn't help with my intentions to gain friends and confidence. It is also one of the very few times I have cried. That is actually something I regret and wish I could change about myself.

It's not healthy to bottle stuff up, but my method in later teenage life was to completely blank stuff out, so I never had the inevitable outburst that just bottling it up would cause.

I really loved that cat and she was a rare positive relationship in my life, so it's a shame as she could have only been about 6.

There is another time I cried around this time, one evening I was playing in the street with Sean, I have no idea how this came about, as it would be out of character for either of us really, but there was a temptingly weak looking wall at the front of some guys house, that (with no clue who instigated this) we decided to kick it down and run away. I do remember it feeling exhilarating in a way, as I sprinted off, but my thoughts were mainly against it.

And despite being a pocket rocket, Sean managed to get collared by the man, which I just saw as I rounded the corner onto the main road.

I snuck back home as quietly as I could in light of my panic and went to my room.

The inevitable knock at the door came and my mum called me down to explain why there was a policeman on the doorstep, and not for Carl or Adam this time. I didn't know what to say but the police officers brilliantly judged "I believe we will have to prosecute, madam" was enough for me to beg that I wouldn't be arrested and I would be good. Nothing more came of it and any details of the aftermath are lost in the mist of time. I think we had to apologise to the man and pay our pocket money for a few weeks for the damage. Overall well handled, with a clear lesson learned for me about the boundaries of my misbehaviour.

If things went at least moderately from that point on, I believe my life would have been 100% different. Like if there were parallel universes, then this one would have to make a near right angle diversion to get into position.

For some reason I can't be sure if Sean even went to the same secondary school in the end. I've plumbed the depths of my brain for any trace of things involving him in class or lunchtimes and he's just not there. But whether he was actually there or not, we still knocked about together after school.

I was not very tall before I was a teenager, but Sean was even smaller in height. But where I was a kind of average, loose body type, he was like a squat little powerhouse. And he could run fast as well, much quicker than me.

Sean had even started going to a gym, at just 11 or 12 years old and I was somehow invited along by him and another lad called Archie (not his real name).

It's not something I was particularly interested in, but went along anyway to see what they did.

I can't say I enjoyed the cold ex-church environment, but the training they did appeared straightforward. They were doing a circuit training routine, which was easy enough to join in with. Sean was a bit stronger than me and used heavier weights for a couple of the exercises, but Archie was younger than us, stick thin and had to take some of mine off, so there was no embarrassment or damage to my ego in that sense.

It seemed like a good idea to do a bit of training, build some muscle and spend time out of the house with friends. There was some kind of joining fee and a weekly subs to pay, which I would have had to get from my parents, along with permission. I don't remember asking or whether there were any issues around this and I seemed to just start going a couple of times a week so it must have been given their approval.

After some time of regularly going to the gym, Archie's older brother Daniel (not his real name) came along, although I only remember seeing him there a few times. There were photos of him in Powerlifting

competitions so I believe he used to be there 6 days a week, where he would train with his Uncle.
Another person whose real name I won't use right now.
So let's just call him Peter.........
and yes, also my abuser.

If you weren't already aware, or hadn't picked up on by this point, this stories darkest period involves childhood sexual abuse. And worse than that, the evil "long game" style of grooming and manipulative torture that borders on modern slavery, wiping out between 7 and 17 years of a young potentially fruitful life and burdening my remaining years with the weight of the aftermath.
That last paragraph sounds ranty and bitter. Good. I am bitter about it. I haven't got over it. Although in recent years I *have* tried to tackle some of my anxieties and lack of self confidence.

But after battling hard to free myself, tentatively at first, before several years later cutting all ties completely, after all that, I still think the hardest thing for me is that I never had a clear moment of closure. Even while in the middle of this experience, one of my biggest fears was that anyone would find out. I was so ashamed that I had allowed myself to get into this situation and that people will know the kind of stuff that went on, that I could only hope to manoeuvre my way out of the situation and never tell anyone about it.

I swore to myself for many years that I would take this information to my grave. Or at worst tell someone on my deathbed.

For now though, back to 1989 for the grim reality of some of my darkest years, which created the horrendous situation that took many years to finally escape.

Chapter Three

**1989 to 1992
Age 13 to 16**

As we continued our visits to the gym, Peter suggested we try out some training for Powerlifting events. There were three lifts in competition, Bench Press, Squat and Deadlift.
So we had to change our routine to suit these exercises, which Peter put together for us.
Nothing untoward ever happened at the gym, they had saunas that I didn't use and I rarely showered there, preferring to go home straight after. Anyone from the outside would see someone giving local kids a hand to do something positive with no hint of suspicion.
Although there was no physical abuse there, I think that is where the mental grooming process began.
Being in a gym at a young age required some personal responsibility but also gave an adult some authority over you in different ways to a teacher. As Archie was a little younger and was Peters nephew, he was bossed about and it was clear he was scared of him.
He always used to say he didn't need to raise a hand as he could punish you just by shouting.
A 25 year old 6'2 powerlifter versus a 10 year old bag of bones was no contest.
This atmosphere began to permeate into our interactions, which seemed to expand quickly over a short period of time.

It wasn't long before we were playing football on the field near his house, or going along to a badminton club once a fortnight.

At some point in this period, Sean started to miss some activities and visit the gym a lot less or stop completely. I don't remember why or if we talked about it, I just seem to realise one day it was always just me and Peter.

The only incident I remember was after finishing football and walking away, me and Sean were spitting, like we'd seen professional footballers do and Peter lost the plot over it, telling us in no uncertain terms that we were never to do that in his presence.

I didn't actually like spitting but did it through a weird peer-pressure reaction, so I just said yeah ok and forgot about it. Sean was more mature than me and knew he didn't have to accept being spoken to like that. I think it was around this time that he did the sensible thing and dropped off the scene.

When it was just the two of us, these activities expanded and included - helping maintain a shed full of fish tanks and a pond, working on a crappy old car that he seemed irrationally proud of, progressing to joining the brass band he was in among other things.

The timeline of these various events is very faint, but a lot of things happened in a period of time before any sexual abuse occurred, which shows the grooming process was very thorough.

All the while it wasn't just building up an innocent looking relationship, the mental grooming was at its height. As soon as the opportunity presented itself, Peter would erupt from his usual easy going demeanour, to an eye-bulging rage while clenching his fists to look more aggressive.

I had seen this before with his nephews, one example being a trip to a theme park, when Archie's playful messing about crossed Peters arbitrary line, resulting in him picking him up and threatening to put him in one of the big bins. It sounded like this had actually happened on a previous occasion and was used as the default warning from then on.

But being in the line of fire yourself was incredibly intimidating, and his manipulative way with words directed your answers to his liking. Saying the wrong thing could escalate the interrogation to the point where his final warning to comply would be counting to 3, punctuating each number with various comments of "you don't want to see me when I get really angry" and "I don't want to have to hurt you".

The only way out of this high pressure situation was to respond with the *correct* answers. It was something I became numb to over time, knowing these were mainly empty threats and how best to reply for the quickest resolution, which was usually complete capitulation. In the end it barely felt like I had my own mind, or that I had to run my thoughts through a sense check before completing them.

There was one time I definitely recall him hitting me to show that he would follow through on these threats. This was much further into the mental web being created, but shows how the pressure was built and demonstrated that it wasn't all just talk. I don't know what instigated the disagreement, but I can picture being sat in his back garden on a bench, with him pacing up and down, visibly getting increasingly more angry. He sat next to me and through gritted teeth tried to question me or force me to answer in the way he wanted, but I either refused or just kept quiet so he swung his arm up and back-fisted me right in the face, causing my lip to split and a fair amount of blood to pour from my mouth.
Somehow within about half an hour of this happening, he had turned it into a kind of joke and tried to laugh it off as nothing serious, probably to cover for the fact he knew it was completely wrong and undeserved. This just added yet another layer of confusion for me, while retaining the desired effect of making me even more concerned of what he was capable of if I didn't "behave".

I even remember writing myself notes to remind me to "THINK!" as I start my day. How twisted is that, for a young teenager to have to be concerned with every action taken and sentence spoken.

And although I had worked out one aspect of this, it took me longer to realise that most of the time this was used to further entangle me in a sick web of mental obstacles.

There were times at the very start of a conversation where I knew that it would conclude with me agreeing to do something I didn't really want to. Or had little interest in at least.

I hadn't acquired the mental capacity to know how to decide exactly what I wanted to do and how to stick to that belief. This led me to being very indecisive and just going along with the dictated approach.

The same technique was used when there was any prospect of me doing something with other friends, which wasn't often. I can still feel the dread when trying to bring up the subject of meeting up with someone outside of school. I know this should be none of his business and I could see who I want, but by this stage he had constructed a mental hold over me so strong that I knew I would have to ask permission first. There was always an easy excuse to create a problem, saying he was going to ask you to help with some task, or band practice for example. After a while I gave up asking as the ice cold atmosphere wasn't worth the effort. I just turned down any invitations as soon as I was asked.

That's the "Isolation" box ticked off on the paedo grooming checklist.

https://childmolestationattorneys.com/how-pedophiles-groom-children-for-molestation/

It's hard to describe how this soft imprisonment came about or how I could still consider him some kind of friend in light of the emotional blackmail type manipulation.

I can only liken it to the thousands of similar "normal" domestic abuse cases in more ordinary situations, where the same effect is seen. Women (and men) can be beaten and verbally abused but even after talking it over with a friend, could often return home at the first opportunity.
So a husband may begin to verbally abuse his wife and over time escalate to physical violence.
Whereas in my case, the mental torment was intentional to pave the way for sexual abuse.

The lead up to this was just as cautious as the earlier grooming actions, with the gym and other physical activities allowing various chances for unsuspicious touching, easily clearing this next hurdle in the paedo guide book.

Another weakness to attack was that Peter made sure he became friendly with my parents. He often took his niece and nephews on days out and an easy route was to invite me to one of these and come to my house to meet my mum and dad and check that it was ok.

And after gaining some trust from the people who should be looking out for me, there was the added bonus of a day trip to a theme park, or zoo which would not only be used as some kind of coercion (Paedo top tip number 4!), but also to reinforce the mental hold over me by using the environment of a supposed fun day out, to inexplicably break out into a rage over some moderate misbehaviour or accidental spill of a drink. Letting you know in no uncertain terms that you were only allowed to mess around to a level he granted, which would alter according to his mood.

These mental gymnastics were tiring and over time I somehow just resigned to putting up with it and minimising things however I could, while enjoying the activities and clubs that it kept me involved in.

I think I knew I was in serious trouble at the point where he randomly turned up on my paper round route, in his Lada car, saying as the weather was bad he would help. Even as a one off I would have thought it was strange, but it became a regular thing. As only a kid, it was me having to keep telling him it was stupid

and likely to cost more in petrol than the pathetic amount I was paid.
I had up to 3 rounds at one point, two in the morning and one after school. I can't say I ever enjoyed them but it seemed the only easy way to get a few quid.

Another little stepping stone was to blend this situation into times where he would pick me up from school. I can't believe that this was actually allowed to happen, without a lot more questioning from teachers, or parents, surely people weren't that naive in 1990.
In some ways it was embarrassing as I had already realised I was in over my head and what other kids might think, but there was an element of enjoyment over driving round in his car blasting a compilation tape of 80s rock hits. Typical predator behaviour, using a positive "reward" to further the grooming process.
The car was also used for threat and intimidation and although I'm struggling to recall a specific example, there were many times where he would drive extremely erratically and dangerously to a point where I seriously thought it would cause a horrific accident. This would often be used after you'd done something "wrong" and many times he would be drunk as well. Just another weapon in the paedo toolbox.

On the subject of weapons, another more subtle intimidation method was that he was a member of a gun club and stored a rifle and pistol in a safe in his bedroom. There was never a time that these were used

as a direct threat, but knowing how unhinged his outbursts could be, it was a worry that he had easy access to guns.
Me and Sean did go to the range once or twice, getting to fire a few guns including a 38 revolver.
Another cool experience / paedophile coercion tactic!

He had greased his way into all areas of my life, to an extent where he was almost more of a father figure than my dad. While my age creeping from 12 through to 16 put us more on a level of "friends".
That's what we had to be considered at even an early stage, friends. I know alarm bells would be ringing if my 13 year old child was spending 60-80% of their time with their 26 year old mate.
This strange age gap and dynamic caused a lot of social and mental anxiety for me, including making me panic when speaking anyone's name.

As he was called Uncle Peter by his nephews, including the eldest Daniel who was about 15 at the time, I found myself in a position where using his first name felt out of place, but I wasn't going to start calling him Uncle Peter.
So I stopped using his name altogether.
And when things progressed to going round to his house for lunch on Saturdays, I had another cringingly awful time with how to refer to Mr Jackson or Phillip and Mrs Jackson, Patricia, or Pat (not their real names).

These two main examples are enough to see that they are the foundations of why I am hesitant when using someone's name or full title.

The next big offensive move took place long enough into our "relationship" that I could barely raise any resistance to this life altering development. It may have started with an opportunistic event, but I am more likely to believe it was a well orchestrated plan. Following a few recent disagreements with his work mates, he had either left, or been sacked from his job at an off-licence. He then proceeded to cause an argument with his parents over the payment of housekeeping and stormed out saying he was leaving. Coincidentally later on turning up, already drunk, to the pub he knew my parents would be in, to tell them his hard luck story.
Within the next day or so, my parents sat me down to ask their 13 year old son if I minded Peter sleeping on my bedroom floor, just for a couple of nights until things calmed down at home.
This shows a deep level of grooming, where my abuser has created a situation for my parents to feel obliged to let him sleep in the same bedroom as their just turned teenage boy.
He had already made sure there were occasions where I had to stay away for a night, with no suspicious activity, before convincing my mum and dad that this was a normal and reasonable thing to do.

And the fact that it was them that asked, put me in a position where if I said No, there would be follow up questions that I didn't want to face at that stage.
The inevitable "mission creep" set in, with a couple of days turning into a week, with the total length of time a mystery to me. Maybe 2 to 3 months?

It was during this opportune time that the first physical touching took place.
I have 99% blocked out whatever mental maze was put in front of me that day, but the result was me being manipulated into a situation of having to touch his penis first, then he would touch mine.
The only way I can think of is that I used to have a very tight foreskin and it caused me some issues, that maybe he became aware of, after sleeping in the same small room for months. So he may have said he would have a look to see if it looked normal or whatever. Assuming this was the case, this "quick touch" was a test and to create a situation where there was some kind of trust bond that would allow him to move on to the next stage with confidence. If the quick touch resulted in me screaming down the house and calling for the police, then it would easily be shaken off with the excuse of looking at a medical issue, and seen as an overreaction. With my parents likely to offer a glowing character reference.

It was during this first time he touched me that I had a familiar sinking realisation…"ok, so that's just another thing that happens from now on". It finally dawned on me that 90% of the time he spoke to me, were little nudges towards the goal of a fully compliant being to perform his wishes. I had noticed it many times before, this sensation of not being in control of some relatively minor direction of my life. But this life changing incident really clarified that I had almost no control over my own life.

I knew immediately that it wasn't going to stop there, while being completely helpless to do anything about it and having zero influence over what might happen next.

I had just been broken down so completely over the preceding couple of years.

I think disassociation must have set in at this stage, as I don't remember the next physical abuse or how it escalated, only that it did progress from that one touch to general sexual abuse.

I have never actually got to the point of seriously considering suicide, but in the months and years following this horrible night, I had a few phrases I would mutter to myself - "I wish I was dead", "Things aren't that bad, if it gets any worse then I can kill myself any time" or "I really can't wait to be dead".

The mental block I have placed on a lot of the sordid details is to be expected. I remember enough of the sexual abuse to know I wouldn't have consented in any normal scenario, like not being a child for a start.

I try not to recall individual instances as it is too upsetting. That would need a different type of therapy, one that I don't think would work for me anyway. To summarise it, with the level of degradation increasing as time passed, it involved a lot of masturbation, oral sex and horrifying attempts at some kind of passionate affection, progressing to weirder things like taking photo's and dressing up in pre-teen light blue underwear, probably similar to when a child forgets their PE kit.
One detail I would like to completely remove from my mind are the words - Stop and Now, used to control and tell me when to let him "finish".

The one boundary that wasn't crossed, that I'm really glad about, is that it never progressed to anal sex. I have a vague memory of him trying one time and it stopping very quickly, after I refused. Be grateful for small mercies I suppose!

How nobody could see there was something wrong happening I don't know.
My character completely changed and the deterioration in school work is clear to see just from my end of year report cards.
Yet not one parent, teacher, relative or friend tried to have a quiet word with me to see if I was ok. I know it wouldn't have taken a lot to confide in a different adult that I trusted, if they approached me in the right way. But it was the usual case where the abuser manipulated

their way into a trusted position first, making you question if there was anyone you could tell that would challenge this otherwise well-liked man that seemed to contribute to the community.
Like a poor man's Jimmy Savile.

I'm not sure of the exact timeline of these events, but I don't think I had much time at secondary school where things were normal.

One very confusing thing happened around the time this 26 year old paedo was sharing my bedroom, he had started to join my mum and dad at the pub more often and even offered to repay the favour of a room by offering to do some renovations at a Nursing Home that they had bought.
The plan was to sell the house and move into the flat above the home. But It was just an open plan space that needed stud walls building. As these various changes took place, my dad quit his job to manage the Home for example, I'd noticed my mum acting weird when Peter was around. During the same time that the worst of my abuse was happening, my guardian was flirting with him and would clearly cheat on my dad given half a chance.
At the height of this, my demented mother passed me a letter and whispered to me to pass it to Peter when I saw him. I waited until I was alone and read this love note, which declared her devotion to him and suggested they run away together. This fucked with my

brain on so many levels as I tried to contemplate how she could be so blind to what was happening to her son while struggling to understand how a clearly gay man could attract such strong female attention.

There had already been a passing incident with Sean's mum, where she was sat on his lap grinding on him until he got hard. He told me about this and said he wanted to have sex with her but he was a virgin, so he didn't want to look stupid.
Another one knocked off the grooming checklist - introducing sexual conversations to break down the child's inhibitions and make them more pliable. This almost textbook level grooming!

So was he gay, bi, just inexperienced, or a gay paedo that didn't want anything to do with these uninvited advances?
The conclusion I have come to is that he is gay, but due to his strict upbringing was ashamed of this and rather than "come out", he would do stuff in secret. But It doesn't excuse being a paedophile or the destruction of a child's life.
At some point I even caught him with gay porn on his computer, which he denied but soon installed a program that hid all your searches and deleted files completely. I don't know if these were adults or children, I didn't have a chance to look and didn't really want to know.

Back to the love letter, I confronted Peter saying that I had read it and he needs to tell her straight that she is deluded. It might have been a perfect way for me to escape my situation, but even as a child I could see this scenario was a complete fantasy.
He must have spoken to her as I don't remember any further dramas after that.

An event I can date that shows a change in my demeanour, is that on arriving at school on 15th April 1989, other kids were talking about some tragedy at the Liverpool match, which turned out to be the Hillsborough disaster. I didn't follow football and going to a game was not something I'd ever thought about, it all seemed a bit detached and surreal to me. My darkening opinion of life can be measured by my shouting around the yard "who was at the game last night then?" laughing. When Steven and Ian Henderson said they were actually there and their dad was badly injured, I still joked about it. I had started to lose any compassion for other people and had a general outlook that the world is a mess anyway, so it would be better if everyone just died.

My way to cope with the struggle of still going to school during this tumultuous time was to front it out with dark humour, while acting childish in a contrived way, but still try not to draw too much attention in class, by just doing well enough to pass exams.

I did meet some of my few friends in this time, where 4 or 5 of us on a similar surreal level created Child-eesh, which is just messing about like a kid, but in a satirical way. I only remember a couple of names, Paul Bennion being one of them. This carried on for maybe two years, but I can only place a small number of good examples. In one English assignment where we had to produce and perform a mock short clip for TV, we wrote a parody of a washing up liquid advert, signing it off with the jingle - "Mild Green, hairy limsquid". We found that hilarious for weeks if not months. I still find myself singing it when washing up sometimes. Another random act of minor rebellion, was when Robert Flaxington joined in maybe the 3rd year, having relocated and been put forward a year. I'm not sure how he got on generally in our school, but in our odd little group we really liked him and even had a Pythonesque period where we devised Bob Club. To honour this near genius that was a year younger than us, we proclaimed he was a Godlike figure, culminating one lunchtime with one of the funnier things we carried out.

Our English teacher, Mr McCarthy was having his lunch in the classroom, which was at the opposite end of the corridor to the small square we used to hang around in until being moved on.

Our grand plan was to hop from our base, chanting Bob! with each jump, heading for McCarthy's room, do one lap around the desks, past our teacher, leaving him bewildered, then out the door and back to the start.

Bob! Bob! Bob! Bob! Bob! Bob!

It went exactly as expected, although I can't remember much of the events following it. Other than because of the mild stir it created, we decided to enter Lord Bob into a mock election that one of the teachers had organised. There must have been a General Election going on and to give a real life example, a position in school was going to be contested by the students.
The funny thing was that our "party" got the most votes, but as an extra lesson it was deemed that our candidate was ineligible as we hadn't registered correctly or maybe late.
This was a win-win for us as we didn't really want to get Bob elected, just mock the system.
I can only really remember Bob's name and one other from this group, Paul.

In Physics class, I sat next to Paul Bennion, or "yon" as he was called by some of his mates.
The main thing I remember about him was that he had an incredible natural talent for anything arty. A simple doodle absent-mindedly created as he listened to Mr Schobers' instructions, was flicked aside and I could spend minutes looking at the intricate pattern he had drawn.
We had a running joke about a superhero called Ego-man, whose only power was the size of his ego, he was actually useless at everything. Paul devised a logo which looked like it could actually be from a comic

book. The points of each letter were elongated into sharp points with little arrowheads.
I'm confident he will have ended up working as a graphic designer or something like a tattoo artist, but doubt I will ever find out.

Paul is a great example of how my private life impacted my every move. We got on well and he liked some cool bands, some that I knew of and others like, Neds Atomic Dustbin whose patch was on his bag, making me curious to find out more.
But no, I knew it was a bad idea to get too friendly and risk the inevitable soul-crushing times I'd have to refuse the offer of calling round after school or something. So I deliberately kept my distance, in this and many other situations. Meaning I missed out on any chance to make some real friends of my own age, that might have been able to help me to see a way out of the quagmire I found myself in.

Some of the names that come to mind during my time at High School are
- Paul Swift
- Bob Flaxington
- Paul Bennion
- George Hill
- Matthew Dunn
- Stephen and Ian Henderson
- Afshin Alipour
- Piers Lough

- Daniel Farrington

That's about it. Seems a short list. I read through my report cards again to try to place myself in each classroom and who I sat next to, but other than Paul B in Physics, I only remember sitting next to Paul Swift, but don't know for which lessons.
I'd love to know what Paul S ended up doing with his life, he was one of the really popular kids in our year and quite clever. I got on well with him and it seems like another friendship that could have been very important for me if I had the chance to become closer.
I went to his house a few times, they lived in a building that used to be the town Museum, it was obvious that they were fairly well off.
The only clear image I have of being there was when his dad came home with an incredibly swollen black eye, after being hit in the face by a cricket ball.
But the relationship was superficial and I never came to be real friends with him.
The vast chasm of difference in our life experiences was shown in a couple of instances. The first being when we were waiting for the bus home from school one Monday afternoon. He was making a big drama out of the fact that he had split up with his girlfriend over the weekend.
I guess we would have been 14 or 15 at the time and the conversation was tailored to make sure you knew they'd been having sex. I remember him singing the Cher song "If I could turn back time" repeatedly, which was quite funny.

The other big difference in our worlds was that he was involved with a group of lads that were experimenting with drugs, with mentions of pills heard as I eavesdropped during music lessons.
I'd lived such a sheltered life that this crowd actually concerned me a bit and I wanted to stay away from them. I had been frightened off anything risky by the hard line rule in my outside life, which might not be a bad thing when it's regarding youngsters and drugs, but I should have had the freedom to find these things out for myself.
Or as Joss Stone says "I've got a right to be wrong" - https://youtu.be/xHVSptF3_G8

I've got a right to be wrong
My mistakes will make me strong
I'm stepping out into the great unknown
I'm feeling wings though I've never flown
I've got a mind of my own
I'm flesh and blood to the bone
I'm not made of stone
Got a right to be wrong
So just leave me alone

I've got a right to be wrong
I've been held down too long
I've got to break free
So I can finally breathe
I've got a right to be wrong
Got to sing my own song

I might be singing out of key
But it sure feels good to me
Got a right to be wrong
So just leave me alone

So another prospective friendship "petered out" so to speak.

I only remember George Hill as he was the "go to" pick for bullies for the whole 5 years, I think even I mildly teased him at times. Sorry George, you didn't deserve it but you didn't do yourself any favours either.

The Dunn family were friends of my brother Adam really, I did get on ok with Matthew, but they were more on Carl and Adams wavelength.
I can't remember many interactions with Matthew and we could have met up once or maybe a number of times.

That about sums up most of the significant events I remember from High School, a time I'll happily forget anyway.

A further barometer of how my emotional state had malfunctioned is when my Nan died in July of 1990. I would have been 14 at the time. I can picture going to visit her in hospital and knowing she was very ill, some weeks before she passed away. I had already started to put up barriers and prepare myself for the inevitable as by this stage I had forcibly shut down all of my emotions. I knew I wouldn't cry and don't think I reacted at all, just carried on about my day. It seemed odd to me that people were so shocked and upset, when I had already accepted this news would come. The only way to deal with my abuse was to numb 100% of my feelings and memories, a tactic that can't be turned on and off easily.

A few weeks before Nan's health began to deteriorate badly, our other Nan was looking after us while mum and dad visited the hospital. On a phone call I overheard her say "she's dead?! ….what….Oh she's in bed!". Embarrassing misunderstandings like that are one of the reasons I really dislike phone calls. Being unable to react to a person visually makes it hard for me to communicate.

Somewhere between the ages of 13 to 16 I had completely submitted to the fact that I had little control over my life, so I lived in a kind of zombie-like mood, just trying not to fall into another well hidden trap to dig myself even deeper.

One slip I made was to ask if Peter had money problems, as I had picked up on some comments made. It turned out that he had maxed out a couple of credit cards, store cards and had bought other items on credit. It added up to around £13,000 I think. Being good with numbers and quite level-headed, I made him do a budget and contact the creditors to agree realistic payment plans. This all worked well and eventually, all his debts were paid off, but by getting myself involved, I helped create another section of this twisted web. And one that dragged on for a few years. The only positive I take from this episode is that my money management has always been on point and I've never been in debt.

Finances were one of the strongest tactics used to gain control over aspects of my life. Despite being in debt and in a part-time low paid job, Peter always maintained the unbelievable notion that he would be a millionaire by 30, with such conviction that it did actually seem a possibility. With a string of poorly thought through ideas lasting a few months at best, it became clear to me that he was totally delusional. One of these leftfield methods was to become a "professional comper", subscribing to Prize Draw Winner magazine and entering hundreds of competitions each month.

This threw up lots of hypothetical situations that could be used to manipulate my life more intricately. So an exciting sounding Safari to Kenya, including £2000 spending money, would later on open up a conversation about starting to save up anyway, for an adventure type holiday, on the off chance that we didn't win.

And a couple of months in, something that was quite rare at that time, a prize draw to win a house. I don't remember if it was for a particular location, or what value it was but the prospect was the perfect set up for a contrived conversation to begin that inevitably concluded with me practically agreeing to save up for a deposit to buy a house.

This was at a stage when I was aware of the weak position I could leave myself in if I didn't think carefully about my answers. And yet even though I clicked quite fast where the discussion would end up, I still couldn't free myself from this verbal entanglement.

Soon after that a joint account was set up where small amounts were deposited every so often, creating another unnatural bond between us with an open-ended timescale.

Alongside these various mental manipulations, it also offered the chance to control more of my time as I had to sit writing out dozens of entry forms and self-addressed envelopes.

There were several school holidays that I spent most days at his house entering competitions, while he was at work, so even my free time wasn't mine.

This steady wave after wave eroding my liberties, made me overly cautious when committing to doing anything, and suspicious of any indication of leading questions. Something I still do to this day.

Joining the brass band was another huge mis-step I made, but I think this happened quite early on, when I wasn't wise to these offhand suggestions actually being a well laid scheme to remove some of my control and dignity.

I liked playing the keyboard and if given the opportunity I'm sure I would have picked up something like guitar or drums really well, if starting young enough.

So the offer to try out a tenor horn and go to band practice appeared interesting, I liked the idea of playing as a group although I'd much rather it was a rock type band.

Even learning how to read basic music pieces takes a lot of practice, never mind actually playing the instrument. But I recall I improved quickly and was soon asked to join in some of the marches and even garden parties. Once more, in this public arena, there was absolutely no sign of what was going on behind closed doors. With another community type activity being perfectly used to hide in plain sight. Just a decent guy doing his bit to get kids involved in something positive.

The regular ties to band practice and almost fortnightly performances also served to subtract a significant chunk of my personal time.

I was extremely ashamed of playing a brass instrument, I just thought, probably correctly, that you would be singled out as a geek and teased over it. I tried hard to avoid any attention, particularly with something that would create a direct link between school and my weird outside life. This association linking my abuse with "taking part" in things has meant that in later life I have remained quite friendless, as I have severe anxiety about joining clubs / courses or generally getting involved with anything.

Even though I really enjoyed taking part in the marches, playing music that I thought sounded great, I dreaded the thought of being spotted by someone from school. I could imagine them walking alongside for the whole time taking the piss. And there would be nothing I could do to evade the situation.

My embarrassment over learning a decent skill was misplaced, it was just a side effect from not wanting to attract any attention. I was so ashamed that I practically tried to float through the last two years of school like a ghost.

However I still always believed that anyone who knew me slightly, would somehow know my dirty secrets or be able to tell by my bitter character that I was being abused.

A big change in my demeanour was that I tried to actively exude unhappiness. I rarely smiled and when presented with some good or exciting news, I would make some quick witted negative response.

If I portrayed a happy lifestyle, I believed people would think I enjoyed what I was going through. I still find it difficult to express real happiness without a lot of inhibition now.

So that is how I lived out the remaining torturous days of my education, like a ghost trying to not be seen by either "friends" or teachers. It had already been decided for me that University and A-Levels were a waste of time. That incursion took place over a short period of anecdotal evidence and coercion before it was "agreed" that it was best to go straight into employment and sign up for some courses to progress.

This must have been around the same time as another ridiculous scheme to get rich quick, betting on horseracing. There were betting systems where you could start off with just £10, placing a £1 bet to start with until you got a run of winners, leading you to a "guaranteed" £1000 in a short space of time.
After several pathetic attempts at this, the next step was to ring one of the dodgy sounding contacts in the Racing Post that promised a tip for a horse that was carefully laid out to win at a decent price. The proposal was that they rang with the selection early on the day of the race and you had to get the best price available, placing a bet for the tipster of an agreed £20 and then whatever you liked for yourself. Amazingly this was successful at first, with the 1st two winning followed by a close unfortunate loss. The next weekends gamble had the sense of heightened attention around it, with the "bet to" amount increasing to £40 and some specific whispers of information that seemed to suggest that it could well be a genuinely fixed race. One of the horses names was even a play on words of the winning jockey and the owner was his uncle.
I'm sure this was either coincidence or a well spun story, but at the time it seemed like a peek into an exciting seedy underworld of fixed races.
This "inside job" produced a winning result at a massive price of 14/1 with the biggest bet that "we" had placed. The urgency around this solid information

led to a scrambling of any available cash to place a stupid amount like £87, with £40 of that generating £600 for the informant as well earnt payment. It also gained the attention of the betting shop manager, who called Peter to one side to say it was obviously an inside tip, due to the odd amount staked, next time could he let him have the info if he agreed to put suspicious bets through without contacting head office as he should.

Needless to say the "tips" went sour rapidly from then on and the profits disappeared. With other "betting system" type attempts carrying on pointlessly.

I would have been about 15 at this time, with another chance to free me from this invisible prison missed. The careers advice at our school was useless, with no fixed lessons and this incident involving our PE teacher Mr Ross. I was disinterested in what he was saying so started looking at a new betting system. While calculating some odds, he caught me and asked me to explain. I blagged my way out of any serious answer, but looking back a quiet word at the end of the lesson could have given me an opportunity for some kind of cry for help.

The only other advice about further education we had was being given a handout that listed a number of suggested professions to suit different abilities, along with the education requirements and approximate salary. Flicking through the pages I found the highest paying position that I was interested in and believed I was capable of, which was a solicitor.

The long term commitment to getting a degree didn't seem to stack up alongside the projected £30,000 annual reward.

I'm aware now that this would have been a very low ball figure and the potential would be more like £50,000 - £100,000+. But at the time even I questioned the sense in spending 5 years or more in full time education, for what appeared to be a moderate living. Obviously the prospect that I could move away to University and live in student accommodation would unravel years of dedicated grooming, so it had already slowly been dealt with during the 4 or 5 years leading up to this point. My resistance was so crushed by then that I actually convinced myself that going to College for A-Levels was a bad idea. This would have been two years in a local 6th Form, where 2 A-Levels would be sufficient to apply for most Universities.

A key point here is that If this had required moving away at 16, I would have done everything in my power to make it happen.

But I couldn't face another two soul destroying years in this neighbourhood, where even more invitations to meet new friends, or even to go to a party, would have to be evaded like I had some kind of lethal contagious disease.

Chapter Four

1992 - 1994
Age 16 to 18

By this time, my parents had sold the house and we had moved into the flat above the Home.
At exactly what stage this happened I'm not sure, but I'd guess I was 15.
What I do know that after a couple of years, as the business was going well they had bought a little cottage nearby for an escape from work. Over time they stayed there more often and eventually moved out, leaving me to share the flat with Carl and his girlfriend who I don't think liked me.
I remember jokingly saying "my parents have finally moved out" when I was 17 which is a solid date for that at least.
It wasn't a comfortable atmosphere, but didn't really make any difference to my life considering the other crap I was wading through.
I'd always hated living there, partly as I had to endure 4 flights of stairs passing through mixtures of food being cooked, general nursing home smells and the overwhelming stink of piss. On at least a twice daily basis.
I didn't want anything to do with the Home as much as my mum tried to involve me in talking to the old residents or joining in with their activities. This came to a head one December as she literally forced me into

the lounge to go around wishing everyone a Happy Christmas. I straight refused and said I don't want anything to do with the Home. She slapped me across the face and said "Oh so you don't want us to leave you anything if we die then" and "this place pays for the roof over your head". That is the only time I remember her hitting me and it didn't really bother me, my emotions were so shut down by then.

While they were still living there, they had started to go to the pub a lot more and get excessively drunk as they always had lock-ins. More often than not they would come back slamming doors and arguing for hours. This escalated to the point where my dad had clearly hit mum as she wore sunglasses for a few days. Rather than stop and check their behaviour, they continued at the same pace and the fights became two way contests, several times leaving both of them with black eyes.

Despite my cold, black heart that had been cultivated over the past few years of abuse, this was something that gave me the same feelings as the times they would argue when we lived in Hertford. I would cower in my bed, covering my ears to try to block out the shouting, the muffled sounds still enough to keep me awake and feeling strangely afraid of something.

I had enough to deal with in my other life.

What I actually did when I left school I don't remember. I know my GCSE grades were just ok, almost all C's across the board, without really trying. This was still enough to pursue further education if I changed my mind, but I think I ended up with no job, trying even more cringe-inducing and lame attempts at small businesses. To get benefits, "we" both had to sign up to a skills course, creating another classroom type situation to shudder through, but with the added bonus of my abuser being right there beside me this time. It was supposed to be an IT diploma, but the only thing it taught me was how to type reasonably quickly.

After this I decided I had to earn some money and found a nice, if very poorly paid job stacking shelves in a fruit and veg shop, with most of my time spent upstairs in the storeroom area.
The manager Abby was in her mid 20's and all the other staff were of a similar age or younger, apart from one nice middle aged lady, Joyce, who always worked on the till. We had quite a laugh upstairs, with the kitchen preparation area and managers office right next to the massive refrigerated stock room.
We always listened to Rock FM (back when it was good) and took 5 minutes out every day to listen to "Toolanize" where the DJ Mike Toolan carried out prank phone calls.
These were probably the most normal times in my life, where I had the first chance to make any real type of friends. However the ever-present shadow of my home life still maintained the forced distance I kept with these new acquaintances. The few early

invitations quickly dried up, when I was asked to go out for drinks, or meet up outside of work and bluntly refused every time.

A weekly thorn in my side was going into work on a Monday and facing the inevitable small talk question of "did you get up to anything at the weekend?". I must have looked like a rabbit in the headlights the first few times, stumbling over my words and mumbling incoherently. I never figured out a believable response even after years of practice. I'm not a good liar.

This didn't go on for too long though as the others stopped asking, no doubt due to the uncomfortable atmosphere I created.

Any simple deviation from my normal routine was used to reinforce the holds on my private life once again. This instance would be at the age of 17 or 18, when I had at least finally started trying to break these binds with a slow, painful but determined effort.

I'd been asked if I would stay a couple of hours late after work one night to help rebrand the window displays, which would have been 4 or 5 of us, probably having a bit of a laugh and more a social occasion than work.

My fear of approaching this subject was sensed immediately, as if by animal instinct and before I had even finished explaining, it was clear there was no way I would be "allowed" to go.

As the grounds for causing a problem over this were so weak and nonsensical, Peters approach was to launch straight to rage mode, shutting down any dialogue and declaring the matter closed.

Generally though, these were good times and any time at work was a welcome respite from my otherwise miserable existence.

My world had become polarised as I reached my late teens, grinding through the indeterminate prison sentence week by week, contrasting with going to work feeling like day release and a taste of freedom. It was around this time (I think I was 17) that I braced myself for some serious mind fuckery, as I had made the decision that I had to put a stop to any and all sexual activity, which had already reduced to being very infrequent. I just didn't know how, or have the confidence to do it yet.

I knew that attempting a clean break would fail, so I intended to use a longer term tactic, knowing that I'd have to make some assurances that we could still remain "friends" and do the same activities.

I was fully aware that my end goal was the complete eradication of him from my life, but the ties were so numerous that breaking away completely was a step a long way down the path I had mapped out.

Some onlookers might assert that all I needed to do was just walk out and cease all contact to escape my imaginary cell. But I'm at peace with knowing I did everything within my power to wrestle free.

I did try to just "walk out" a couple of times, with each ending in failure and an even stronger belief that death was the only way out.

On an early attempt I was ill-prepared and simply tried to ignore and avoid him, from which I was easily whipped back into line in a matter of days. But another more carefully laid plan involved me quitting all of my paper rounds and just declaring that I was free. I remember riding my bike around wherever I liked, it was raining and I truly felt like a freshly released prisoner, so ecstatic to have escaped these chains.

But somehow after less than a week the binds began to reattach, with my psyche completely drained by this point. If I couldn't make a clean break, then unfortunately I would have to take the long route out, or end it myself if things got too tough along the way.

It's hard to get across in writing how all consuming an abusive relationship like this can be, but I hope I've gone some way to doing it justice. Or maybe I should have just grown some balls, punched him in the face and said "Don't come near me again you nonce". The next ten years would have been a lot simpler if I had done so.

I must have worked at the fruit and veg shop for about 18 months and this was almost the first time in my life that I had been able to just chat to either male or female "friends" without oversight. And inevitably it is

finally time for a girl to enter the scene. I think more out of circumstance than attraction, I started to get along well with Melanie (not her real name), who was a similar age to me and worked at the fruit and veg shop part time to support her college lifestyle.
She developed a crush on me and despite my social awkwardness I managed to act quite naturally around her, buoyed in confidence by the unusual position of being liked by a female.
Over time, I somehow built up the courage to ask if she fancied going for a drink after work.
Being only 17 I decided to "borrow" my brother's driving licence and even so, the barmaid clearly knew I was underage. She must have taken pity on this awkward kid obviously trying to impress his date by taking her to the pub, as she served the "beer" I had hesitantly requested, but only half a pint to let me know I'd been rumbled.
We sat down and had an uncomfortable, stilted conversation, with me desperately trying to steer clear of any subjects that might uncover the other side of my life.
I don't think we stayed long, thankfully she suggested going to her house for some food, where I found it easier to talk a bit more.
We saw each other a fair number of times, but it's hard to place a length of time on this "relationship". We must have been considered boyfriend and girlfriend, as I remember having to break up, and we did have some minor sexual activity.
But it didn't feel like a proper relationship.

The weight of my troubles made that impossible, with the intensity only increasing as my captor could see I was attempting to break free of the mental web he'd spent years creating.

Any interactions were fraught during this period, with a stormy atmosphere lasting days setting in if there was the slightest inkling that "your giiirlfriend" might get in the way of some previously agreed event. In one outburst following a heated discussion a day earlier, he waited until I was at work, then drove up and down the street a couple of times and blasted the excessively loud air horn that he had installed.

Yeah, like a full on stalker.

The combination of relentless pressure and realisation that my new relationship was more due to convenience than attraction, brought my first "romantic" episode to an end.

It was just easier to resign once more and return to my familiar cell and warden, for the time being.

It did at least fortify my efforts to cement the fact that our "friendship" was purely that.

I definitely grew from this experience and quickly made progress, which is when I had the confidence to confront Peter and put an end to any sexual activity. I nearly bottled it and initially agreed to his proposal that everything would stop completely, if it could be phased out slowly.

This cursed dilemma reveals how sick this individual is, while highlighting how desperate I was by actually accepting this premise.

Within a few days, I rescinded my "deal", having finally recognised the power I held in this situation. And then everything did stop, with no further attempts that I remember. I was so happy to have finally won a small victory and establish a position that would last. My elation wouldn't last long, with the even larger issue of disassociating myself completely seeming like an impossibility.
If abuse was my cell in solitary, then friendship was a towering prison wall, with searchlights and snipers.

If anything, the next large slice of my life that was destroyed was the most surreal and socially excruciating. Potentially a further 10 years of entrapment, lessening in the final years before ceasing completely.
You would think that a paedophile would want to cut their losses at that point, with age and a maturing attitude cancelling out the prerequisite aim of the relationship.
And the key fact that I'm not gay, or bi. I've never had homosexual feelings in all my years.
I know the feeling of attraction to women, and men just don't do it for me.

Fuck knows the reasoning, but this only galvanised the efforts to tie us together in as many ways as possible. This gradually morphed into having an unexplainable 24/7 relationship as platonic friends, with no females in the picture. To anyone looking at this set up, would appear to be a straightforward gay couple, with a questionable age difference of late teens to mid 30's.

Chapter Five

**1994 to 1997
Age 18 to 21**

Next stop on this runaway train was to randomly quit my job and set off on a trip to France, hoping to find work in a ski resort and stay as long as "we" could. The mild insanity with this plan is a good barometer of the level of desperation to hold on to power by this stage. Having saved up a pathetic £1000, this was deemed sufficient to last a few weeks until waltzing into a job. Needless to say, it didn't pan out like that. The "wild camping" turned into a night in a hotel and after getting a bus to a ski resort, it turned out there was little snow and we were told to return in a few weeks as the season hadn't started.

After finding the cheapest chalet available, the finances were already looking low.

We would be struggling to stay more than a week or so and I somehow got talked into asking my mum for a loan. I hadn't got on well with her for a while and along with the surreal situation and the fact I hate borrowing money, this all added up to a difficult conversation.

She agreed to send £1000 to my account, but she must have heard the despondency in my voice, I'll never understand why she never made efforts to check that I was ok.

To keep piling on the embarrassment with this adventure, the snow never came and the trip was cut short, turning into basically a rubbish, very expensive 2 or 3 week holiday.

Trying to stretch funds where possible, the "sensible" decision was taken to walk back down the mountain, instead of waiting 4 hours for the bus. Naively we thought it would be easy to scramble down the green slopes, cutting the distance of the road dramatically. Fences and uncrossable bushes quickly put an end to that idea.

To add insult to injury, we still had to get the same bus that came from the ski resort and the amount saved on the journey was minimal.

The cherry on top of this shit-cake was a visit to EuroDisney on the way home, the crap version of Disney World. All in all another new episode to be completely ashamed of.

These next few years are a blur, with no real order to the events in my mind.

I believe "we" got a placement at a stables, to be able to continue claiming benefits.

It was to complete an NVQ level 3 in stable management, which was a two year course. This mainly consisted of nearly full time general yard work, with an hour or two theory lesson and an hour riding each day.

Another double-edged sword situation, as I've always wanted to work with horses, but not with the shadow of my home life creeping around my every move.

The staff were mainly female and all quite fun loving, enjoying the yard work with music playing and having a laugh. In other circumstances this would have been a good environment to knock my personality back into something like normal shape.
Needless to say it was another 2 years of uncomfortable conversations and semi-friendships that I could do nothing to progress.

Chapter Six

1997 - 2003
Age - 21 to 27

Off on another wild tangent here, at what exact point in the story I'm not sure, but somehow out of the blue, my dad was accused of rape.
After a few years of successfully running the care home, they had organised a very popular annual garden party, which on this occasion ended with a very drunken night and an after party in the flat.
The next morning one of the staff had gone to the police and claimed my dad had pinned her down and raped her. My dad was many things, but in my opinion definitely not a rapist.
I'd guess they were all too drunk to know what they were doing and while my mum was passed out in their bedroom, this left an employee in her early 20's and my 50 year old father alone.
Not that this is any kind of justification, just a statement of what happened.
Whether it was consensual can never be proved to me, but I don't think my dad would force himself on someone that was saying No. If that was the case then he fully deserved to be prosecuted.
I had become so detached from my family at this stage that I barely paid attention to what was going on. I never went to any court hearings or asked what was happening. I'm not even sure of a lot of the details.
All I know is that he was eventually found guilty and

given maybe 5 or 6 years, likely to be out in 3 with good behaviour.
I did finally manage to visit him a couple of times towards the end of his sentence.

The next chapter I can recall is applying for jobs at a betting firm who had a few shops in the area. Being jobless again, "we" both applied with the rationale being that there would be a good chance one of us would get an interview. They turned out to be desperate for staff and took us both on.
Another fine mess you've gotten us into!
Starting as a part time cashier, I quickly completed all the manager training so I could cover shifts in other shops and take manager shifts for longer hours and better pay.
This period was less horrendous as we would rarely be working in the same shop.
I enjoyed the job and there weren't many people I worked with that were of a similar age, so conversations would be mainly small talk and reasonably comfortable for me to be friendly.
I worked for this company for 5 years, before moving on to work for a different operator.

So the time had come to reap the rewards of the long-ago seeded plan to buy a house. After finding stable employment and finally clearing every last bit of debt, the idea of moving away and buying a house was re-introduced.

I was so sick of the town I lived in by now that the idea actually appealed to me, anything for a chance of some kind of clean slate. I believe this would be around the year 2000.

After looking at house prices in some ok places, the best area looked to be from the Preston to Kendal area.

Being unable to afford a deposit for a house straight away, we moved 60 miles north, but somehow ended up renting a static caravan on someone's farm for a few months first.

Perfect, a fresh start with new people to deal with and I live in a caravan with my older "housemate". This reduced my confidence even lower and made me even more anxious to keep any conversations away from home life.

And many more horrific episodes of "Did you do anything good at the weekend?"

Within a short period of time working around all the shops in the area, it was clear that other staff assumed we were a gay couple.

This compounded my feelings of desperation and inability to socialise as I still couldn't talk openly with these new acquaintances and make any real friends.

We did eventually buy a house at about £40,000, just before the housing market boomed.

Probably the only good fortune I'd had in years.

But the large catch to this forward step was the obvious escalation in "connection", at a time when I was pushing hard to expand my freedoms.
It really started to feel that it might take me a lifetime to free myself from this all consuming oppression.

I did at least manage to go out for the occasional staff night out, with one pub crawl resulting in a good conversation with a lass called Michele.
She had her own horse and seemed to be really nice, so we swapped numbers and planned to meet up.
I can't remember if we even managed one date, I definitely never went to the stables and don't think we went out for a drink. The only incident I can picture is when I returned home and parked my car in the garage, only to see Peter come out raging about something.
It might not have been overtly because I'd arranged a date, but it was clear to me that was the issue.
This was probably the closest he got to ever actually beating me up, with the peak being him smashing his fists, with keys held downward into the bonnet of my car leaving a few dents and scratches.
Whatever followed this outburst, I backed off from meeting up with Michele, out of embarrassment rather than fear.
I would have been around 25 at the time. I honestly thought I'd broken past this point by now, so it was quite shattering.

What exact mind-games were used I'm not sure, but I'd always been put off learning to drive until around this time. So having only recently passed my test, getting a car at the age of about 25 was quite liberating and did give me some sense of my own freedom. Each little taste of liberty was satisfying but also increased my desire for more.

As a marker of my mental health at this stage, I used to love driving fast with the music blasting and it made me happy, but I had started to wonder if I could just swerve into an oncoming truck and end it all really quickly. I hate to think of how many times this thought crossed my mind. .

The next surreal turn was that my dad was allowed out on bail, awaiting sentencing but with conditions that he couldn't stay anywhere in the town where the care home was.

This resulted in him asking us if he could stay in the house for this probable 3 month period.

I was so confused by this stage, as I had lost nearly all contact with my family so it was a strange atmosphere for a start. But I also believed he wasn't guilty of this harsh crime and it did upset me that this was happening. I worried about the life he would see me living, where I was visibly depressed 90% of the time and if he would try to find out if I was ok.

We had no choice but to let him live with us, or he would have to stay in prison.

The interactions weren't as uncomfortable as I thought, mainly on account of my dad being holed up in his room, only popping down when necessary. I'm sure he was genuinely just trying to keep out of the way to not intrude on our daily lives. To me I felt there would have been an opportunity for my dad to pull me to one side and have a serious chat, but this never happened. One misfortunate coincidence was that [Peter] had to stay away with work for a night, so I seized the chance and arranged to go into some pubs in town. This was the first chance I'd had to have no-one peering over my shoulder at every move and knowing I could come back to a paedo-free house.

I remember my dad seeming unhappy about something at the time, but I was too excited to snatch a small piece of freedom while I could.

Later on he did say that he had been hoping to have a chat as it was the first time [Peter] hadn't been there. Maybe this would have been the "intervention" that broke the spell and shortened my sentence. Bit late at that stage anyway, but it would have been nice to have an honest talk with my dad.

I was so severely detached from his situation that I honestly can't say what happened when he left our place. I don't know if it's that he was off to prison to serve his term, or if I've misremembered the reason he stayed with us in the first place.

My best guess is that yes, he was on bail and the next step was prison, with another development to come in a few years when he was near to being released.

Following the Michele incident and the unexplainable reaction, I knew I had to act, so some time after I told him I wanted to rent my own place, in the same small town and he could buy me out for half the value of the house.

This was a big move and I had (maybe foolishly) watched my step to make sure I could pull it off. It took a few months but I was determined to follow through this time.

I compromised by staying in the same area, rather than moving to the city where I could put some distance between us and have the chance to go out into town easily any time I liked. Instead it was a £15 taxi fare each way, making nights out an expensive luxury. Maybe I should have had the courage to just make a clean break at this point, but my previous failed attempts haunted me. So I played it safe and at least now had my own private space to use as a barrier while I tried to re-integrate into society.

This tactic did work and was the start of the final stretch of my road to freedom. Within a year I had moved to rent a house on the edge of the city and soon after that managed to buy my own place on the next street along.

At this stage in the book, I am unsure if the picture that I've painted is harsh enough to warrant my long term compliance. I could go into great detail to explain the daily manipulative grooming that led me to continue to be confined in what was "only" a manufactured prison of my mind.

But I know I did all I could and now that I am completely free, it is time to move on, which I hope to achieve by writing Volume One.

That is the best way I can try to gain the closure that has so far escaped me, as I gradually breached my parole conditions further and further, I just reduced contact slowly over time, until eventually only visiting every few months for a "catch up".

This meant that there was no specific end to what was a peculiar relationship and one I'd rather forget. I didn't get my day in court, or a fiery argument resulting in a complete and immediate detachment. As I've said, I didn't want anyone to ever know, so I just played it that we had always just been sharing a house to split costs until we found our own places. But enough had happened in my outside life that was inevitably tainted by this period of my life that I could never fully escape the shadow it cast.

I wish I'd addressed this earlier in my life, but I didn't see the problem while in the middle of the storm. I have made steady progress now though and am looking forward to putting the final nails in the coffin of my previous life by completing this project.

Chapter Seven

2003 - 2007
Age - 27 to 31

During this period, I jumped ship to another betting operator and had 2 years working in the shops before getting a promotion to work at head office.
While I was in the shops, Peter had taken a trainee area manager job at the original firm, but obviously couldn't cope and was taking a lot of time off sick with some mysterious high blood pressure issues that were blown out of all proportion. He claimed to have some rare condition that meant he could collapse at any given moment, but I think it was just stress from being a disgusting paedophile.
He got fired or left within a few months of this and would you believe it, a job came up at the new company I'd moved to.
Just as I had started to finally branch out on my own properly, the cringe-inducing presence of my former life was there to knock my confidence once more.
When I started working at head office it did at least give me another minor chance to start with a clean slate, but immediately the slate was muddied as one of my main colleagues used to work in the same area of shops as I did.
To my other colleagues, I should have come across as a young, single guy with a decent job and a bachelor pad, but there was always a question mark hanging in

the air when one particular work-mate was involved in the conversation. I'm not sure how much he knew, but I would occasionally be asked "What's that guy doing now that you used to live with?"

Another senior manager that I knew well also had to deal with him after he was off sick long term and he also occasionally questioned me for updates.

I really did have very little to do with him Peter by that point, but these interjections were enough to show I still hadn't been able to make a clean break, even after a 10 year struggle.

In some aspects I feel that there is a similarity to when someone decides to "come out" as gay, where they feel a massive relief and can start a new chapter to their life. I often wonder how different my life would be if I'd had the courage to "come out" as having suffered years of abuse, gone to the police and saw him prosecuted, which would have given me a point of closure.

But I am so ashamed of every part of that period of my life that I convinced myself it would be better if nobody ever knew the truth.

It was only years later that I realised that I could never be truly happy until I opened up about it, tried to address it and then finally move on.

Still, I soldiered on and the new job actually turned out to be the biggest and best change to my life so far, despite the doubts I had. I had to travel about 1000 miles every week all over the country, staying in nice hotels and going out for meals. It was a demanding job, but really rewarding and we lived by the clichéd motto "work hard, play hard".

I had an overbearing sense that people questioned my sexuality, so I over-compensated in the next few years, making sure that all of the small group of "alpha male" workmates (not me, still beta for a while) knew that I was always trying to get girls back to the hotel room when we were staying away. The others were just as bad, but I was always trying to one-up them.

The reckless behaviour I pursued for that 3 year spell is what I should have been doing in my late teens, not my late 20's.

But I am a believer that there is no harm to come from someone having a wild period in their life, to get it out of the system before settling down later on. I don't regret anything and we had a great time, although there are a couple of things I would do differently with the benefit of hindsight. Ok, maybe more than a couple ;-)

Finally I was starting to manifest some of the "coming of age" events that I had missed out on earlier in life. It was during this period that I did finally have my first proper girlfriend, Serena (not her real name) and we had a fun couple of years, maybe it was 18 months. She was someone I met through work and her brother became, and still is, my best friend.

There wasn't a clearly distinguishable beginning to this relationship, we just seemed to end up being on nights out with a group of people from the shops a few weeks in a row and eventually some unspoken agreement left us in the position of being "a couple".

We went out quite a lot, to pubs and clubs and even travelled abroad for holiday, loads more "normality" milestones passed, albeit belatedly.

I was still firmly entrenched in the positions that "long-term relationships don't work" and "bringing a kid into this world is a bad idea", I think understandably so, given my lived experience of the world.
I put up a hard front when it came to relationships, making it clear to Serena and any other girl I was seeing that it was nothing serious and just a bit of fun.

Despite starting to carve out a more normal and outgoing life, the effects of nearly two decades of mental torture were hard to fully overcome.
Outwardly, I had spent so many years consciously trying to look unhappy with the world, that I couldn't (and still can't) avoid this particular expression in a lot of situations.
Yep it makes me look grumpy. In my current life, Taylor says I scowl at her all the time, but luckily she kind of likes it.
There was a great quote by Alex Turner (Arctic Monkeys) in a magazine interview where he said "I'm not miserable, it's just me face", which eventually got printed on a T-shirt for me!

My negative attitude would increase whenever the discussion of children came up, with my standard response to the question "What would you do if I found out I was pregnant?", being   "Push you down the stairs, obviously". I only half meant it, but have always been really careful not to end up in that position unwittingly.

Even though I had started going out with "friends" and now had a partner, I still struggled to know how to act in most social situations. I found it hard to make conversation, always waiting for other people to talk and then chip in with witty side remarks.
My girlfriend must have thought I was strange, or at least that's what I felt at the time. She had some knowledge of my background as we worked in adjacent groups of shops when we met, so we sometimes had to cover shifts in each other's area. Maybe nothing seemed odd to her, but I still never knew what to say when she asked about this guy that people talked about.

Overall, it was a decent first attempt at a more responsible relationship, but after about a year or so I realised that I was not going to be happy in the long term. We had talked it over a couple of times and attempted a "fresh start" approach, but these efforts gradually slipped back into the same issues we were having earlier.
Eventually it ended on a bit of a sour note as I basically said "It's not working any more, I'm going away for a few days, if you could move all your stuff out by the time I'm back."

I was going to Germany to watch England play in the World Cup, through some tie-in with work and this seemed as good a time as any to make a bold decision. I had learnt that if I want to get out of a situation that has developed into something I hadn't intended, then I have to act decisively, however harsh it might be.

I had just turned 30 when I brought this relationship to a close, which gave me another new lease of "freedom" to spread my wings. Psychologically, I was still very messed up, but began to push myself to do more new things and try to make some friends. Other than casual workmates, I had precisely zero actual friends which is something I continued to struggle with (and still do).

I'd started to find it a lot easier to talk to girls, with the obvious goal of trying to line up a date or exchange numbers. Where I found it difficult to speak to other guys, as being 30 years old, most people around my age had already established their groups of friends and I always felt like a bit of an outsider. Along with my general awkwardness, the continued niggle of wanting to shake off any doubts about my sexuality caused me to shy away from starting conversations about arranging to meet up for drinks with other lads. I know this is irrational but it was a strange dynamic where I'd be the odd one out around a group of mates, just waiting for some kind of invitation to join them next time they went out round town, or had a poker night or something.

So even though I was now in a decent job with good conditions and having a really adventurous time with work, I still wasn't happy. The novelty of going out drinking and trying to pull when staying away for work wore off after a while and due to some regulatory changes, our jobs altered quite a bit where we were more office based for a while and the team had reduced to 4 or 5 people.

I had used my work situation as a crutch and a bit of a bridge to get me back into something resembling a normal life, but still found myself sat at home alone most weekends wondering what I was doing with my life.

One outlet I started to explore was to go to live music gigs, the first actually being the day after I returned from my short Germany trip. I'd signed up to a load of bands email newsletters and while away, had a message about a short notice "secret gig" by Dirty Pretty Things. I replied to the invite and had received further instructions to follow for where and how to collect my ticket.

This band was set up by Carl Barat soon after the breakup of the Libertines, who I was quite fanatical about at the time, so it all seemed pretty special and exciting. And the good thing about a gig is that it didn't matter that I had no friends to go with as once you were there in a crowd of people bouncing around, you could be there on your own or in a group of 10 mates and no one would know the difference. I loved the chaotic atmosphere of the very small venue and even managed to chat to a couple of people at various times through the night, learning a new trick of blocking one ear off with your thumb, as it actually made it easier to hear someone talking over the raucous audience and pounding of guitars and drums.

Throughout some of my darkest years, one of the only escapes I had was music. This was one aspect of my life that I could actually control, as there was no way to stop me listening to what I liked and I made a conscious effort not to let Peter know what that was, as some minor act of rebellion along with not wanting to have yet another area of my existence corrupted by his influence. I used to sit in my bedroom and listen to a few different radio stations and make my own mix-tapes of random songs I liked, at first being drawn in to the Britpop craze with bands like Ash, Pulp, Blur, Elastica and Space. Ash quickly became a clear favourite, with their Nu-Clear sounds album being etched in my mind from countless times of listening to it from start to finish. A combination of heavy rock, dark and moody songs, with a couple of heartfelt melodic tunes in stark contrast, in the space of 11 tracks it provided me ways to vent some emotion and express how I was feeling. A couple of songs can demonstrate this and sum the album up pretty well.

Death Trip 21 -
https://www.youtube.com/watch?v=ZJwzGjftYow

You got a taste

*You're playing with the dark stuff
Don't let it get under your skin
The world's overpopulated
Fucked up anyway
You'd hate to think you were missing the fun
You got a taste you're playing with the dark stuff
Don't let it get under your skin
I seen your eyes in the bottom of my glass
You died in your sleep
Your face incomplete*

Folk Song - https://www.youtube.com/watch?v=XAfHxPdMK8E&list=OLAK5uy_lYfTdj_Y_v5SCIOdX_A4qmOcmhg0bPWfo&index=6

*Walking through this changing season
Sorrow spreads its wings
We can't keep a hold on time
Just receive what it will bring*
After the great night I'd had at my first gig, one of the next that came along was the chance to see Ash in an absolutely tiny venue, upstairs at 53 Degrees in Preston, with a capacity of just 300. I got my ticket as soon as they went on sale, not even concerned about seeing if anyone else was interested, and going alone again. It was another fantastic night, I pushed my way right to the front barriers and stayed there all night. A lass near me had a flashing LED belt that you could program your own message to appear on; she opted for

"Play Girl from Mars!!!", kind of pointlessly as it was their biggest single, so they obviously would at some point.

Regardless, she was doing her best to get the bands attention at the end of each song, eventually taking it off to wave about as high as she could. As she was quite short, I offered to try for her and, probably just due to the song appearing next on their setlist, the lead singer made some comment about it, so I passed it back and they had a bit of banter with her then burst into a great live version of this iconic song. It's unique interactions like this that make any live gig, but especially small ones, so much fun to be a part of.

Around the same time, Arctic Monkeys were just about to release their second album and had planned some warm up gigs at tiny venues. I'd been following them from even before their debut album was released, buying a couple of homemade CD compilations of their demo's off eBay. I was aware that Serena's brother was also a fan and this was an easy way for me to strike up a bit of a friendship, as we swapped CD's and talked about how amazingly well written the lyrics were.

So as soon as I heard that they were booked to play at the Dome in Morecambe, I got in touch with Mark and we made plans to meet up and make sure we got tickets. The band obviously knew the demand would be massively higher than the number of tickets available (less than 1,000 definitely, but may have been more like 500) and they'd already had previous experience of ticket resellers snapping them all up immediately, just to scam massive profits from genuine fans. So in order to claim a ticket, you had to queue up at the venue box office the morning before the gig, with tickets going on sale at 9am. I think we got there at about 6am, not at the front of the line like some crazies who'd literally camped from the night before, but comfortably close enough to know that we wouldn't miss out. Being level headed and good at planning, I turned up with fold up chairs, a backpack full of snacks, drinks and even speakers to get some music playing while we waited. Initially feeling a bit over-prepared, nerdy and not very "rock 'n roll", these insecurities quickly disappeared as the rest of the queue shuffled about awkwardly or sat on the floor desperately wishing the time to pass as quickly as possible. While we had a brilliant morning, chilling in our comfy seats, hearing the jealous comments about our great set up and even starting to take requests for the next songs we'd play. It turned the whole experience into a memorable weekend that I'll never forget.

I've even managed to find a short video that I took on my (Nokia) phone during the gig, which is very poor quality but clear enough to hear that it's during "Teddy Picker". The visual reminder really helped bring back memories of us repeatedly crowd-surfing our way to the front, getting dragged over the barriers by security and bundled back out into the bouncing crowd.

I'm sure that at 30 years of age I could be considered a bit old for these kinds of antics, but these were the first times in my life that I'd actually started to lose my inhibitions in some circumstances.

These amazing early gig experiences left me addicted and over the following years I attended many concerts and festivals, no longer having to skulk around on my own as I had a new wingman to accompany me, pretty much my first real friend, who is still my best mate today.
I do feel like there are a couple of big obstacles that have got in the way of us developing a really close friendship though, one being that he lives an hour drive away and not exactly in a conveniently accessible location. This has meant a lack of opportunity to just knock around together and see each other on a frequent basis, with most of our get-togethers being for specific events like the numerous gigs or maybe birthdays and other occasions.
The other invisible wedge has always been the skeletons in my closet, as I've never given any indication of the issues I've been through. I'm sure he knows there were some complications in my youth, due to my various social issues, but again I've preferred to maintain a distance around my past and keep away from any serious open conversations. It feels like an all or nothing situation to me, as the events of my earlier life are so extreme that it's not possible to tell some of my story without explaining everything to give it the correct context.

It will be interesting to have a good chat after he has read this and I'm sure it will strengthen our relationship and give us a closer bond.

As I began to piece my own life back together, I made some efforts to reconnect with my dad.
I think he had a year or so left of his sentence when I arranged to visit him for the first time. I had been writing letters to him for a while and looking through the replies I received again now makes uncomfortable reading, but it did at least pave the way for some reconciliation.
One development that happened quite soon after my dad was sent to prison, was that mum started going out with the new landlord of their local pub. I wasn't really aware of what was going on but my brothers seemed to detest this new man on the scene as they believed he was taking advantage of the situation and knew my mum would likely have quite a bit of money if she got divorced.
From a young age I had the impression my parents weren't happy together, but the truth is that my dad was content, if a little complacent and in the usual marriage rut, where my mum was really not happy and felt "trapped" in a relationship, as can easily happen. However, the manner and speed at which she seemingly dropped her husband to take up her new life was harsh and I think affected dad seriously. The fracture this caused in our family was severe and still continues, as far as I know my mum doesn't keep in touch with either Carl or Adam or her grandchildren.

About five years ago I also stopped contact with her, as there was rarely anything positive to come from times I would visit and I had started to begrudge the lack of awareness and action taken during the critical earlier times in my life.

I broke off our relationship with a long text message, alluding to the fact that I wasn't happy with how she had acted, but not with any specific information of why. At this point, if she had made some real effort to talk things through and see what the problem was, I think there is a chance I would have opened up to her about my abuse and we could have worked through it. But her reply, if there was one, was of little note and left me under no illusion that she was not concerned about losing touch, or attempting to resolve any issues. I haven't spoken to her since then.

So the letters from my dad eventually revealed that their divorce was final, with mum receiving the lion's share of the settlement, dad having been in a very weak position to negotiate.

It was soon after this that I visited him in prison, which was a very strange and uncomfortable meeting, but again some progress.

Another cruel twist in his story happened around this time, with a diagnosis of cancer making his final months in prison even more dire.

When he was released he rented a flat near the seafront and had a year or two of various treatments to try to eradicate the cancer, but managed to live a relatively normal life and have some fun at least.

I tried to visit any time I was working in the area, usually meeting up for lunch every month or two. Despite the severe circumstances in both our lives, I don't feel we ever became that close, it was quite a surface level relationship and the conversations were mainly small talk.

But at least we had developed some kind of friendship while it was possible.

As the disease took its toll and it became more a case of "when" not "if" he would die from it, there were a couple of family holidays planned, just a few nights away at a lodge, mainly fishing.

My brothers were there with their girlfriends, one with kids and I went with Serena. They were good times and everyone had a laugh although I still felt a sense of detachment from my close family.

When he became really ill, dad moved to stay with his oldest brother in South Wales, as they had a spare room and could look after him well.

It was really difficult to arrange to visit there due to the distance and my work being in opposite areas of the country, but I managed it a few times.

One of my biggest regrets is that on the last visit I remember, it was clear he didn't have long left, I had the urge to open up about some things, but really didn't know where to start and the opportunity didn't present itself, so we just bumbled through the usual small talk type chat and I left with a casual "see you next time" atmosphere.

A few days later Adam phoned telling me to come and visit as soon as possible.

I don't remember where exactly, but I was away on business and probably could have dropped everything to go immediately, instead of delaying until the next day, as I did.

As I pulled up outside the house, both of my brothers were there and it was obvious that my dad had already passed away and only quite recently. I don't know if I would have said anything different, him being on his literal deathbed, but it will always upset me that I wasn't there for him right at the end. And that I hadn't pushed myself harder to open up on the previous visit. That is something I would like to change as I grow older, as immediately someone actually dies, it really is final.

As the saying goes, everyone's life is so busy these days that we only meet up for "weddings and funerals", which is quite accurate for our scattered family.

My dad's funeral was at least an opportunity for me to present some kind of normal front to my life, attending with my semi long term girlfriend (although I think we had actually broken up by this point).

We gave him a good send off and the obligatory drunken wake, exaggerated by the heavy drinking culture of South Wales (not knocking it!).

My dad's side of the family have always been very outwardly emotional and all of his 5 brothers and one sister had stories to tell that would end in someone crying or being visibly upset.

My years of personal struggles had built up many layers of stone around my heart that has made it near impossible for me to express any emotion, happy or sad, so I was consistently matter of fact throughout this time. At the end of a long nights drinking (therefore the details are vague) my uncle (dads youngest brother) started to question me quite strongly about why I didn't seem bothered that my dad had died, which resulted in some kind of argument and my parting shot being a punch to his stomach as I tried to evade this uncomfortable discussion.

I did get a bit upset after that, so I suppose it served its purpose in the end.

I can't say I went through any long term grieving process, my attitude with death is that it comes to us all and particularly when someone has a terminal illness, by the time they die I have already processed those feelings and quickly return to "normal" life.

I do think about him quite often now as I get older; his age of death at 57 seeming so very young and a shame I couldn't get to know him better over the next 20 years or so.

Chapter Eight

2007 - 2011
Age - 31 to 35

After continuing to play the field a little while longer, albeit at a slower pace, I had started to come around to the idea of having another steady girlfriend, but due to my preconception of how long term relationships pan out, I was going to be very picky about who that might be. Or as I coarsely put it, I want a decent test drive before I make a purchase!
And while I had consciously made a bit of a mental shift, my defence mechanism would be to outwardly keep things very casual, until I'd had plenty of chance to weigh up the situation fully.

As I was driving across to the other side of the country to take some photos of one of our shops, I was on the phone to a colleague who said "I've been to that shop Davo, you'll like the lass in there, feisty blond chick with cracking boobs!!" I laughed this off and expected that it would be a different member of staff working to when he'd visited.
As luck would have it though, Taylor was in the shop, and he was correct on all counts!

The work that should really have taken about 20 minutes, ended up stretching to nearly two hours, as we had a right laugh and neither of us could stop talking for most of the time.

We had a lot in common, initially I asked if she knew of any decent poker tournaments in the area, which quite unusually for a girl was something she was also interested in.

This led onto chats about bands and festivals, with her reeling off many of the same heavy metal and rock bands that I had started to get into.

As I completed my work chores, I said I may need to come back in a few weeks to follow up, which was genuinely the case, but I wanted to make sure she was aware so I could try and see her again.

Yes, my first instinct was that she was hot and I wanted to get her into bed, but even on this first meeting I felt there was something slightly different and that we had some kind of connection.

I think she had a two week holiday booked and sometime after that I did get in touch again, arranging to meet up for a drink outside of work. After that first night out, where we got on really well again, we started to meet up at least once a month, going to concerts or out in her local town for fancy dress parties or other random nights.

All the while I still maintained a frosty stance towards any committed relationship, to continue my tentative progress with less sense of pressure. Fortunately Taylor was also just coming out of a long term relationship, which I believe began to come to an end following events during her recent holiday. So we were both in a situation where we didn't want anything too serious, but had also got the majority of our wild times behind us.

Another helpful factor during this early period was the physical distance between us, as she lived nearly a two hour drive away. And she doesn't drive. She would happily get two busses and two trains to see me though, which was good.

Where this may be a problem for a lot of relationships, it actually helped us both to get to know each other and acclimatise to the situation without things becoming too serious too quickly.

As the time passed and we did start to get closer, my fears of commitment kicked back in and I had to deliberately try to outwardly portray that this was just a casual affair, while internally I knew it was more important to me than that.

The times spent together were definitely more like a couple in love than just a physical relationship, but that four letter word - love - would be enough to make me run a mile even at that stage. From our first meeting in 2007, we had had so many great times over the next four years, cramming in more fun than I had managed in the preceding 30 years of my life, but I still wanted the best of both worlds. I was happy with this set up, acting like a happy couple for the frequent times we were together while still having space at home to do my own thing.

I'd made it clear to Taylor all along that I hate long term relationships and don't believe they work, so it is completely understandable that as time went on she had to make some sort of decision to suit her own situation.

We'd had a good time, but knowing that this would never turn into anything serious, she had started chatting with a guy that fancied her. Not that I was fully aware at the time, but they had been on one or two dates and there was a good possibility that she could have scaled down our relationship and moved on to be with someone that was more likely to want something more settled.

Around this time we had arranged for Taylor to visit for a full week leading up to the August Bank Holiday weekend, with loads of fun things planned. We'd booked a meal at a French restaurant where we both wanted to try lobster for the first time, we were going to visit Chester for some shopping, a wander around the cool old streets and City Walls, followed by a stay in a nice hotel for the night. Then back home I'd booked tickets for a Burlesque night at a pub in town which we accompanied with several bottles of prosecco.

Despite the busy itinerary and the good time we had, I had picked up on some slight feelings of distance between us through the week, also noticing that Tay was distracted by her mobile phone a little more than normal. My instincts were correct and by the end of the week when we were at the Burlesque, it was clear that it was another man turning her head, which forced me to confront my own feelings directly.

The potential threat of this amazing relationship that we had built up just fizzling out made me realise that I had to decide, after a thorough four year test drive, whether I wanted to commit to this model or not.

Supported by the dutch courage of prosecco, when we got back to my house I took the opportunity and asked Taylor if she would be my girlfriend. I had done such a thorough job of marking out the boundaries of my relationship expectations, that she practically went into a state of shock, believing that I had only said this due to being drunk or as some kind of joke! "Ask me again in the morning if you're serious" she said, and while I happily went to sleep, she apparently was unable to, having a sleepless night of questioning and thinking about her own situation.

As soon as I was awake she brought the conversation back up, saying "Well, anything to say?", I said "Oh yeah, that, yeah I was just joking", before quickly reassuring her that I wasn't really and asking again if she wanted to be in a more serious relationship with me and be my actual girlfriend.

Of course she said yes, but there definitely remained an undercurrent of doubt in her mind for a while after, due to how definitive I had always been up to that point.

I'm sure after knowing me for four years she was aware I had been through some issues in my life, but I doubt it was to the extent of the reality. It would still be another five years before I spoke to her openly about my past, but I'm certain that had she known these details at the time she would understand my fears around taking, what was for me, a massive step forward.

Although on face value there had been quite a seismic shift in my life, in practice it didn't result in any immediate major changes to our lifestyles. We already had other events lined up and tickets to gigs booked for the last couple of months of 2011 and continued to meet up regularly. In hindsight, I suppose the more destructive path would have been taken if I hadn't picked up on the unintentional subconscious hints that Tay had given me during that pivotal week.
If I really had just wanted to continue our long term "friends with benefits" non-committal relationship indefinitely, then there is a high likelihood that she would have looked elsewhere for the stability and security that is inevitably needed as you get a little older.
Not that there was any pressure from her side for me to come to any decision about this, quite the opposite. I'd stated (and reinforced) my stance on relationships very clearly and Tay respected that position and never tried to "trap" me in the ways that a lot of girls do when they have the urge to tie a man down. In fact, it is me that is now jokingly accused of doing the seduction and laying of traps, with Tay highlighting all the moves I'd pulled, inviting her for a week filled with romantic gestures of days out, expensive hotels, intimate meals and nicely finished off with a drunken

evening watching a light-hearted sexy show, before hitting her with the killer question! I can honestly say that this was not the planned intention, it just worked out that way, but I am massively grateful that it did. Had we drifted apart at this juncture of my life I really don't know what I would be doing now.

Chapter Nine

2011 - 2013
Age - 35 to 37

The initial months of our new "honeymoon period" as a proper couple did lead to an increase in the amount of time we wanted to spend together, with visits becoming every other weekend and additional nights wherever possible. The distance wasn't necessarily a problem but it did gradually become frustrating as we had now pretty much reached the limit of how often we could meet up. It did at least confirm that stepping up to an "official" relationship was the right thing to do as neither of us had serious second thoughts about the decision.

We had our first full Christmas together with a couple of days spent at my house before travelling down to Kent to see my Auntie for New Year, which has become a bit of a tradition now.
The festive season has never been a happy time for me, for obvious reasons as a teenager through to my late twenties. But even most of the years following had been uncomfortable, as I tried to worm my way into parties and nights out with friends that I didn't really have. The self-induced distance I had put between myself and most of my family meant that it was

generally quite a lonely time. I guess no more than usual really, but accentuated by the general social expectations around this period of the year.

I can definitively say that I'd grown to hate Christmas and it was always a relief to me when things went back to normal in early January.

It had now also become an instance where Tay would ask what I usually liked to do at this time, or what I remember about Christmas when I was younger. She loves Christmas and likes to make it special by stocking up on certain drinks and snacks, as well as watching favourite films and doing other things that "remind you of good times you had as a kid".

My go to response of "I really just don't remember" wasn't a complete lie. Partly I just didn't want to recall any of the intensely uncomfortable situations, while my knack of totally blacking out other memories did the rest of the work.

But in spite of my negativity and literal "Bah Humbug" message on the black and white Santa style hat I wore, we had a brilliant time and it was one of the first Christmases that I had enjoyed in many years. Another good indicator that my life was finally starting to move in a positive direction.

The new year continued in a similar pattern to the previous, meeting up as often as was physically possible and booking gigs and festivals to look forward to in the months ahead.

One amazing opportunity that we'd managed to get tickets for was to see Shinedown in the relatively small

Manchester Academy venue, with a capacity of around 2,000. These were a band that we had both only recently become aware of and one of the first times where we discovered some new music together that really impacted our lives. I think it's fascinating when you stumble across a great band that have been around for years but you've either never heard of them or somehow overlooked them previously. All of a sudden you're presented with three or four albums worth of incredible music and mind-blowing lyrics that you just can't understand how you've missed all these years. An early stand out track that we both loved was the acoustic version of "45", with its heart wrenching lyrics being belted out with such power that you can tell comes from a place of genuine emotion. Tay would have gone to the gig just to see Brent Smith perform this song on it's own.

https://www.youtube.com/watch?v=PD_D23yDBPU

By chance the concert happened to be taking place on February 14th, not that we were trying to book something for Valentine's Day, but it was a happy coincidence. It also ended up being the first time that I'd ever told someone that I loved them, at the tender age of 35!
As it was on a Tuesday night I was driving back straight after the gig, so it's not even like it was due to being drunk. Just another step forward on the path of a more normal life.

As anyone that has been in a long-distance relationship will know, it's not that the inconvenience of travelling detracts from the situation as such, but over time it just begins to make more sense to look at the ways you might make changes as things progress. At some point following the Shinedown gig we talked about the idea of moving in together and after discussing the possibilities, Taylor moved in with me by the end of July.

Although I had some negative thoughts about the place I lived, I do actually really like the area and owned my own house that I was keen to hold on to. It was also ideally placed geographically considering that my work might take me to Scotland one day and Birmingham the next.
In contrast, Tay was at a point where she was quite happy to consider relocating for a fresh start, having a few concerns about her hometown and no doubt uncomfortable bits of her own history to break away from. It wasn't a clear cut decision, as she comes from a very close knit family that all still live in close proximity, which would be a massive compromise for her to move away from.
The opportunity of a transfer to a shop in the area came up and the decision was made, a big development for both of us.

For logical reasons I had always tried to keep my home life private from either casual friends or workmates, but even I didn't mind letting some information slip out about my most recent news. It definitely felt like I was edging ever closer to something resembling "normal" and for the first time in my life I wasn't crushed with complete shame and embarrassment when a conversation turned in that direction.

It did lead to the inevitable semi-teasing banter of "You'll be married with kids next!", as anyone that knows me is well aware of my cold hard stance on these subjects over the years. No thanks, just living with someone again was enough for me to take on at this time.

I was still so mentally scarred and irrationally afraid of any commitment that when the time came for Tay to actually move in, I panicked and drafted up a list of "house rules" that I felt would help me cope with the inevitable alterations in my day to day life. I had lived on my own for the last 8 years and even though I had instigated the change to this, my involuntary defence instincts kicked in as I worried about a possible loss of control over my life once more.

It is a bit embarrassing that I compelled my girlfriend to "sign up" to these terms and conditions and I cringe about it thinking back now. My own concerns also blinded me to the fact that I was putting in place something that would be considered very controlling of someone that I was supposed to be entering into a trusting relationship with, quite hypocritical considering the earlier traumas in my life. But overall I believe it was something I had to do as a sort of support crutch to help me transition into this next phase of my life.

Although I think she was a bit taken aback and maybe even a little hurt by my odd request, Tay took it in her stride and responded in kind, with her own list of "boyfriend rules" to comply with. Touché!

Over time I learnt that in order to help a relationship work, both parties just have to compromise with some things and find ways to get along, without the need for a list of rules.

Chapter Ten

2013 to 2014
Age - 37 to 38

After cautiously tip-toeing forward every step of the way in my newly liberated early 30's, the changes and progress in my life picked up pace exponentially as I got closer to the "big 4-0".
We really enjoyed living together and after a few months I was confident that we could have many happy years as a couple, enough so that I suggested we should keep an eye out for a house to buy together. The idea was to see what properties were coming up for sale over the next year or so and get a feeling for where would be a nice area to live. Over this time we would also build up knowledge of the going rate for houses in our price range and make sure we had enough saved up for a deposit so we could act decisively when the time came.

When I bought my current house it took me several months and many different viewings to find something suitable, so I was fully expecting it to be at least a year until we were faced with a serious decision to make. We had made a list of "must have" and "nice to have" features, which although not very demanding, it can take some time for all these various points to fall into place.

As it happens, within just 2 or 3 days I had stumbled across a fantastic opportunity that I felt we couldn't pass up. At very least it deserved a viewing to try to understand why this unusual property was on the market for quite a low price.

I've always liked the idea of living somewhere where the garden isn't overlooked by neighbours, but being realistic I knew I could never afford the sort of detached property that would be required for this luxury. Despite being an end of terrace house, the main appeal of this house for me was that there was a massive garden, which runs right alongside a canal for about 60 feet and is cut off at the bottom end by a bridge, where a rear driveway connects to the road behind the house. The layout gives it a very secluded feeling, even though it is effectively in an area of a small housing estate. There is also a nice view of the canal from most rooms, particularly the kitchen, conservatory and two of the bedrooms.

The reason for the affordable price quickly became clear when being shown around, as every room was in desperate need of redecoration and all through the house, windows and external doors needed to be replaced. My opinion was that this was a once in a lifetime opportunity, even taking into account the poor condition and potential cost of turning it into a comfortable place to live.

Taylor was more apprehensive and for a couple of reasons didn't have the same level of interest as me. For one thing, wherever there are midges or other insects, she is usually mauled by them and has bad reactions to bites, so living next to a canal wasn't a massive plus point in her book. She also hates the disruption of building works while trying to get on with normal day to day life, so the thoughts of taking on somewhere that needed a lot of attention was a major barrier. It still wasn't a "no" for her, just a much lower level of enthusiasm than mine.

As a form of compromise, it was decided that we'd make an offer at quite a bit below the asking price, then if we were outbid that was fair enough, at least we'd tried. We weren't going to get involved in a bidding war, as we didn't think that it was worth the full asking price. Having spent the last 10 years working hard and making myself financially secure, we were in the position to proceed on a "no chain" basis, so could use this as a little leverage to keep the price down.

Also if we could secure it for a low enough amount, I would be able to keep hold of my existing property, meaning we could live there until the main disruptive works were completed. Then later on we'd have the option to try renting that house out when we moved to the new one.

Once we had made our offer and mentally committed to the idea, the feelings of anxiety that quickly kicked in confirmed that we'd both really love to live there. We talked about what we'd do if the response was that they would only accept the "asking price", or that another party had exceeded our offer and we tried to put a realistic ceiling on the maximum we would go to.

I rode my bike along the canal past the property a couple of times in the next week to have a look from a different perspective and really started to appreciate what a unique little house it was, making me even more concerned that someone would come along and gazump us.

I began to imagine the situation where we had missed out and were back to square one of looking at all the houses for sale, picturing all the "normal" 2-up 2-down type properties that we would likely be going to view, with a small garden and neighbours over the fence on either side giving me an unusual version of claustrophobia. That clearly comes from psychological issues where I have a strong desire for privacy so that nobody knows anything about my life. Even though I had been "free" for at least a decade by this point and had now started to create a decent world for myself, the damage that had been caused still weighed heavily in my mind.

Luckily from that point things moved quite fast, as the sellers appeared to want a quick sale and were in a similar "no chain" situation, which is unusual in my experience. Their counter-offer was at a level pretty much halfway between the asking price and our offer. There was a temptation to try to knock another one or two thousand off, but the wise decision was made to just get the deal agreed and put an end to any worries of missing out.

Everything went smoothly and in a matter of a few months we had signed up to a joint mortgage and were ready to collect the keys.

This was the first chance we had to have a proper look around this empty property that we were hoping to make into a happy and welcoming home together. There was definitely a lot of work that needed to be completed before it would feel homely, but being able to leave everywhere like a building site and return to the other house did make it much more bearable. The next couple of months were spent non-stop decorating and having old things ripped out and fresh ones installed, at times feeling like there would be no end to this process. But we got there, with another relationship test passed as we avoided any serious arguments during this stressful period!

When we'd had the chance to give all the rooms a thorough clean, most of the construction type work was complete, and our bedroom was nicely decorated, we decided to stay in the house for the first time overnight.

To celebrate I had picked up a bottle of Champagne on my way to collect Tay, before heading to our little nest, as we'd started to call it.

Finally being able to fully relax in the home we had created together was such a massive relief and as the evening went on I could tell that we were going to be really happy here, it just felt perfect.

After a couple of glasses of bubbly, chatting about all the changes we'd made and how nice the house was looking now, I got Tay to come out into the garden to see what a lovely little place we had. Standing under the moonlight, looking around our garden and across the canal with its pretty little bridge, I did something that I never thought would have been possible in my entire existence and asked her if she would marry me. I hadn't planned to do this and didn't have a ring, but I was quite happy to let her choose her own anyway. Of course she said yes and it was a really nice memorable moment to share together, with the fact that Tay was wearing a giraffe onesie at the time being the main thing she likes to remind me about!

So from the age of 35 when for the first time in my life I had lowered my barriers just enough to profess my feelings for someone, in the space of 18 months I was now engaged and living in a jointly owned house. And I was completely content with how things were progressing.

I guess it was kind of a quick journey, but we had been seeing each other for four years before anything became serious, which suited us both at the time. Pretty much as soon as thoughts of marriage had entered my head, I had popped the question at the first opportunity. I knew it was going to be the right thing to do in the long run, so why wait.

One thing that really grates on me is when people get into a relationship and after a certain period of time, those around them start to repeatedly ask, "so, when are you getting married then?". It just seems to take any spontaneity out of the circumstances and almost make it seem like an inevitability or that you've somehow been "worn down" until *reluctantly* doing the right thing.

This may be an incorrect and cynical view of the situation, but if I was going to get married I wanted it to be 100% clear that it was of my own volition and my fiancée to have no insecurity about my intentions being genuine, rather than it being out of some kind of feeling of duty.

I believe I achieved this goal and was confident that my wife-to-be truly understood that this proposition meant that I wanted to be with her for the rest of our lives.

By the end of 2013 we were spending our first Christmas together as a happily engaged couple.

We had no particular timescale in mind to get married, or grand ideas of an elaborate wedding day. We knew it would happen at some point and that was enough to put us both in a comfortable, secure mindset for the foreseeable future.

Chapter Eleven

**2014 to 2015
Age 38 to 39**

Even though we were both clearly settling down a bit now, it was important to us that we didn't gradually slide into the common problem that blights many long term relationships, the dreaded "rut". Nights out to gigs continued as often as possible, although stand-up comedy replaced a lot of the rock bands as time went on, an indicator of our ages ticking upwards I guess. We also liked to go to quirky towns, random castles or other oddities all over the UK. My job still required me to cover a large area and I would build up a list of interesting spots I'd noticed on my travels that we would plan to visit when we had the chance. From some of our earliest trips away together, I'd made a habit of getting a fridge magnet to help me remember places we had been, as I knew my brain was still conditioned to actively try not to hold on to memories. We've now nearly completely covered the fridge with mini-adventures!

As seems to generally be the way with life, when things are going well there is no doubt something likely to come along and knock you back down to earth.

In August of 2014 we were having a great time at a strange little "shepherds hut" that we had booked for a few nights in Kenilworth. It was like a tiny caravan and really cosy, with a view of Kenilworth Castle right outside, which we even attempted to do a little watercolour painting of. Neither of us are particularly arty and didn't have a clue what we were doing but still both managed quite a respectable effort and a relaxing, fun afternoon regardless. We spent the rest of our time exploring the area, which has a very rich history, even appearing in the Domesday Book that was compiled in 1086 by order of William the Conqueror.

At some point in this short break away, Tay got a text message that despite having no specific information of any problem, the tone instinctively told her something was wrong. As soon as we were back home there was a phone call that confirmed her fears, with the devastating news that her dad had been diagnosed with some form of cancer.

Not only was this a massive shock, it just didn't seem to make any sense at all as he was one of the fittest people you could meet. He was only 57 and would start most days with a 20 - 30 mile bike ride, up and down the hills of Northumberland.

Always approaching life with a very positive mental attitude, if anyone could beat this it would be him. The next 12 months were impossibly difficult for everyone involved, with the initial determination and efforts to remain upbeat gradually being worn down as each attempt at treatment failed to make any major breakthrough.

As he lived in quite a remote region over 2 hours drive from our house, short visits weren't ideal so I would often drop Taylor off and return a few days later. I would usually only be there for a short period of time and even in those few minutes my incompetence for normal human interaction was evident. My benchmark lack of social skills was magnified by the added complexity of the situation and I could barely do little more than sit there fiddling with my phone or make the occasional clumsy smalltalk.

For some reason I feel more at ease making conversation in situations where I am just one on one with somebody, so when this scenario cropped up and I found myself sat in the room alone with Tays now quite frail dad, I noticeably felt my conscience twinge as if to give me a nudge into action. Clear in my mind was the time I had spent at my own fathers bedside and my subsequent feelings of regret at not having managed to talk openly with him while I had the chance. Taylors dad wasn't exactly on his deathbed at this point, but I believe we had now arranged our wedding in the hope that he could be there to walk his daughter down the aisle. I can't say that we had a long, deep and meaningful talk, but the words we did exchange were very worthwhile with my stated promise to him that "I will look after her you know, when we're married" being all that I can specifically remember. I hope it gave him some comfort that his little girl was in safe hands and I am glad to have at least had this connection with a man that I didn't get to know as well as I would have liked.

As can be gathered from my description of this period, Tays dad never recovered from his illness, passing away almost exactly a year after being first diagnosed, with his wife and my fiancée caring for him full time for the last few months. Having seen him deteriorate and being there during such a horrific time took its toll and in hindsight I think Taylor suffered with PTSD symptoms for at least a couple of years following his death. It turns out that he had encountered asbestos during one of his jobs and this had caused irreparable damage to his lungs.

We had decided to plan our wedding quite quickly with the aim that he would be well enough to attend by that time.

As is fitting for our dark-humour cloaked personalities, we thought it would be interesting to get married on 31st October and we planned a fancy dress "Hallowedding". Unfortunately he passed away in mid-August, which added its own sombre tinge to the proceedings, but it is still a day we both enjoyed and will always remember.

Actually, I'm not sure I can say that I fully enjoyed it. I was very happy to "be" married but not really a fan of the process of "getting" married.

I still struggle immensely in any situation where I am the centre of attention, having spent most of my life trying to attract as little attention as possible. So the thoughts of having this Big Day that was all about us primarily filled me with dread rather than excitement. One of our original plans was to take a holiday to Las

Vegas and return with the news that we'd had the clichéd "shotgun wedding", which would have suited me perfectly.

The changes in circumstances meant that we had to have something in the realms of a normal wedding and given the gravity of the situation even I accepted that. We did make sure it was a long way from "traditional" and the adjustments certainly made the whole experience more bearable for me. For a start we didn't have a long service in a church to endure, in fact we had the absolute shortest version of the vows that we could muster and it was officiated over by a cheerful guy dressed as a vampire!

The guests were also all in Halloween fancy dress for our ceremony, which makes the photographs hilarious to look through. I wore a nice black suit and Tay looked amazing in her purple wedding dress, flanked by 2 bridesmaids all in black. We got changed into our Gothic King and Queen outfits afterwards, ready for the fun part of the day.

We avoided having a sit-down meal and any speeches; the thought of having a Best Man speech alone was enough to be a deal-breaker for me.

Everyone went straight from the ceremony to the reception venue to get drunk and have a buffet. There was no first dance and even though we had planned to do a "cutting of the cake" to add at least some formality to the evening, even this got missed in the heat of the moment.

Looking at these details now I'm sure a lot of people would say that we had removed most of the best parts of a wedding, but if I was getting married again today I would want the same set up. In fact I know I still couldn't cope with all the bells and whistles of a full-on traditional wedding, showing once again how deeply entrenched my psychological problems are. Looking on the bright side though, I had made such progress that I was now happily married, just before I hit my 40's and had the wedding ring to prove it….black, of course!

Chapter Twelve

**2015 to 2016
Age - 39 to 40**

I thought it was quite funny when I went back into the office for work on the Monday after our wedding, as up to that point none of my colleagues were even aware that I had been engaged for the last 2 years, such was the level of my personal privacy.
I knew someone would notice my ring, as I never wear any jewellery, and I hate being on the back foot in a conversation like that so I wanted to be the one to bring the subject up. I had brought some of the wedding cake in and made a point of offering it around, watching the bewilderment as these people that had known me for over a decade and who *knew* that I'd never get married, find out that I had done just that.
Another example of slightly odd behaviour, but the only way I knew how to cope with the situation.

With that socially awkward hurdle successfully cleared, things kind of settled back down to normal. We didn't have a honeymoon straight away and being a married couple wouldn't materially change anything about our day to day lives, so it really was a case of "business as usual" for the time being. Over the next couple of months I went through a sort of re-evaluation of my life, inevitably I suppose, having just got married and fast approaching the landmark age of 40. On one hand I was astounded at how far I had come, from literally being in a place where I couldn't perceive a way to escape and wished my life would end as soon as possible, to a point where I had a gorgeous wife, lived in an amazing little house and had a well paid job that I mostly enjoyed.

On the other hand, I still couldn't shake the background radiation of depression that hung over me, while social interactions continued to be a struggle and to top it off, the ever persistent niggle of Misophonia to deal with.

"What will it take to make you happy?" I repeatedly questioned myself. I kept coming back to the same issue as always, the lack of closure following my abuse.

The more I thought about it, the more it added up to a lose-lose situation. If I take this information to my grave I don't think I can ever be content, but the concept of going to the police at this stage seemed to be an even worse solution. So if I couldn't get actual closure, what about talking to someone about it or having some kind of counselling. I couldn't handle seeing a psychiatrist at that stage and the only person in the world that I could possibly confide in was my wife, who I didn't think I could ever tell unless it was on my deathbed, such is the level of shame I feel. What if it changed the way she felt about me, or she saw red and hunted down my abuser; these were just two of many irrational scenarios that I envisaged.

After doing a bit of online research I eventually decided to ring the NAPAC helpline (National Association for People Abused in Childhood - https://napac.org.uk 0808 801 0331), a call I put off several times before actually going through with it. This would be the first time I had told anyone about my abuse or even spoken the words out loud, but the call handler made it very easy and gave great advice. Overall, it was just so relieving to talk to someone about my past honestly and I came off the call feeling a lot happier and knowing that at some point I would have the courage to tell Taylor about my tragic past.

I didn't take too long to make this next step, but to give myself the confidence to talk to her about it, I had booked a hotel about half an hour away, making out that we were just going out for a meal and a change of scenery.
My actual plan was to create a situation where I couldn't bottle out of tackling the subject, within a neutral environment where I'd be more comfortable to talk and there would be no homely reminders of this life changing conversation.
My wife knows me well and could tell something was amiss, so we never actually got to the stage of leaving the house, I just said what I needed to say and we had a strange week of additional little chats. My worry that she might have second thoughts about our relationship was completely misplaced. She couldn't have made me feel any more secure and clear that she was open to listening without any pressure of what details to

divulge. Enough was said at this time to explain most of what I wanted Tay to know, so it can be safely left unmentioned without any adverse effects. There are occasionally times when the subject comes up and I don't mind talking about it, as it helps me look at how far I've come.

Talking about my past has helped me immensely. As time has passed, I have eventually told a number of people my story and felt the weight lifting noticeably on each occasion. But the feeling of a lack of closure remains, maybe even increasing as I come to terms with the events I've lived through. It was during the next phase of my life that I began to seriously think about putting these thoughts down on paper.

Chapter Thirteen

**2016 to 2019
Age - 40 to 43**

The job that I had been doing since 2004 had shifted and changed over the last few years and it was clear to me that the future was not very secure in this department. I had started to keep my eye out for any other opportunities, either externally or for promotion within the company and eventually in the latter half of 2016 I secured a position as the Product Manager for a part of the business that I knew had a lot of potential for growth in the coming years.

Apart from the considerations I had about my existing job becoming less stable, for the last couple of years there had been a growing desire for me to have another fresh start. Ideally this would involve me leaving for a completely new company but as this hadn't transpired, I was satisfied that this new post would give me the opportunity that I'd been looking for. It's hard to explain the dynamics of the head office building that I worked at, but in short the small department that I'd been in for the last 12 years was somehow segregated, both physically and culturally, from the main part of the business. We dealt with the owner of the company directly, where everyone else answered to the managing director. So my move over to the "other side" was like a soft version of starting with a new employer, where I would be interacting with different people in my day to day work. The only slight complication to this was that my boss for the last few years had recently been promoted himself and was now the CEO and the person that I would be reporting to.

At this stage of my life I truly did believe that being able to start afresh could give me just the kick-start I needed to finally move on from my troubled past and evolve into a positive, confident Alpha male and even build some new relationships that could be classed as friends.

This new job would require me to be the head of my department, ok this consisted of me alone, so it's not like I had staff working under me, but I did have some level of authority when dealing with other sections of the business at least. And I would be attending monthly board meetings where I'd have to present reports to a room of 10 to 15 other senior managers. I tackled these challenges head on, working hard and making various improvements that saw positive results within the first few months. Although it was far from perfect, I could feel my self-confidence improving as I began to settle into this more demanding role. Some of the departments were particularly difficult to deal with, Marketing just seemed to make every interaction as painful as possible and IT never managed to help me out a lot, although not for a lack of trying in their case. But these tests of my developing new character were taken in stride and if anything only added to my overall positive outlook of how things were going.

For some reason at just the time I felt I'd really turned a corner, the CEO appeared to go out of his way to publicly undermine and belittle me whenever the opportunity arose.

The clearest example would be at a quarterly meeting, where the head of each department had to give an update on all aspects of their work. I had worked hard non-stop for the couple of months leading up to this, improving every facet of my department and the business levels I presented highlighted this really well.

I have always desperately struggled with any public speaking, but my growing confidence allowed me to give a decent presentation for once. As I sat down breathing a sigh of relief the only response was from the CEO, which was to say "Right, heard enough of that, let's move on the stuff that makes the money".

I'm well aware this was probably only said in jest, or banter, but in one sentence he had managed to negate everything that I'd toiled over since taking on this job. To do this in a boardroom full of the most senior staff just completely undermined me and squashed back down any confidence that I'd slowly managed to build up.

Following this, there were a number of similar snide comments made when in the presence of other staff, such that over time I lost all motivation for the constantly stressful job that I was doing.

And as I battled on, trying to do my best while anticipating the next verbal attack on my fragile mindset, I realised this wasn't a new trait that the head of the company was displaying. He had always made scathing comments and tried to raise himself up by belittling others, only before that time it hadn't caught my attention. This was partly because I was now in a "head of department" position, which placed me more directly in the firing line, while the progress I'd made in my private life caused me to look more objectively at how other people treated me.

As I thought about it more, I realised that there were elements of my work life that resembled some of the same abusive behaviour that I'd had to deal with earlier in my life.

Obviously not at anything like the same scale, but similar patterns of behaviour occurred where I'd have several positive interactions over a short period of time, getting on well with my boss and feeling that a sense of mutual respect was building. Then as I was starting to relax and drop my guard I would be cut down to size during a high profile situation when the opportunity arose.

I felt as if I was encountering a lightweight version of the grooming that I'd suffered as a child and I knew it wouldn't be healthy to continue on this path in the long term.

I still completed 3 years in that role, seeing annual turnover quadruple from around £40m to £160m, but these early knocks to my confidence were enough to confirm that I needed to find a way to leave the company completely and have a real fresh start in life.

One potential new beginning was falling into place nicely by the middle of 2019, as Taylor had recently completed a diploma in Floristry and we were in the process of buying a running business. Having achieved a Distinction for her college work, we were confident that she could take over the workload from the previous owner, assuming there was a reasonable handover to ensure the level of service was maintained while she settled in. There was also a part-time member of staff who was an excellent florist and was held in high regard locally.

We had looked at florists for sale all over the UK and it was difficult to find something that met our requirements, then after about 9 months of searching, just as we were losing hope, a great little shop was put on the market in our hometown.

The asking price was over our intended budget, but there were so many benefits to this opportunity that it was worth pulling out all the stops. The fact that the shop was only a couple of miles from our house would save thousands of pounds, a lot of uncertainty and stress in comparison to all the other businesses we had looked at.

We made an offer which was accepted and solicitors were instructed to start proceedings as we worked through various details. Everything was moving forward reasonably well with a couple of issues remaining that should easily have been resolved by meeting with the sellers.

We began to get excited about this new challenge and talked through many different plans to make improvements to the running of the business, but the focus was on ensuring the transition period was as smooth as possible so that there was no major disruption to the sales and income during this period. Tay was going to run the shop along with the existing staff, while I continued to work full time until we were comfortable that the business levels were reliable. Over time we intended to expand the customer base and increase the workload to a point where it would make sense for me to quit my job and take over all the management aspects of the shop, while also helping out and doing the deliveries. This would free Taylor up to concentrate on the practical floristry side and target higher profile events and weddings.

I could picture an end in sight and a time where I would finally be able to leave the company I'd worked at for many years, breaking free from some of the last remaining skeletons in closets that still tainted my life somehow. To a certain extent I had mentally prepared myself that I would be resigning in the coming months, which had the effect of reducing my motivation even further while also confirming that it was the right decision, as I began to look at the overall situation from a more distanced perspective.

As the weeks ticked by and the deal solidified to the point where we needed to start considering an actual Completion Date, the minor outstanding issues were still yet to be resolved and rather than crossing things off our To Do list, a couple of more crucial problems raised their heads.

Halfway into the process, when official documents were being shuffled back and forth between solicitors, it came to our attention that on top of the sale price for the business the seller had listed an amount for "Stock" of £10,000. Our view was that this was an artificially high value as the only stock being held would be the live flowers that should be being used and replaced every few days, likely amounting to a few hundred pounds. We tried to question this directly but by this stage the seller would only communicate via the solicitors, which made every step slow and overly complicated. We were informed that the stock included many items that were used for weddings and other events.

This had never been discussed during negotiations, just added in when contracts were drawn up, so our response to the solicitors was that we didn't require any stock of this nature, only the things needed for the general business. We attempted to arrange a visit to take a look and see if there was a way to resolve this point, but having to send messages via both solicitors every time was making it difficult. The only way we could proceed was to say that we would look at instructing an independent stock taker to list everything at the point of completion and then decide what additional items, if any, that we would take ownership of.

Unfortunately this wasn't acceptable to the seller, whose attitude was that we had no choice but to accept everything, as there wouldn't be enough time for them to sell things off before the deal completed. This stumbling block refused to be smoothed over, but didn't stop the overall progress as on its own it shouldn't have been enough to be a deal breaker.

A much more important question that we had been trying to get a sensible answer to was relating to the handover process. As we were paying a decent amount of money for the rights to the business, it was important that everything was done to ensure there was minimal disruption to the day to day running of the shop and service to regular customers.
This should have been easily and amicably covered by our suggestion that Tay would work in the shop alongside the existing staff for a week or so, being shown the basics of any systems they had in place, introduction to any corporate clients or repeat customers and generally any peculiarities of how this independent business was run.
We were told a straight "No", she wouldn't allow us to do that as the other staff weren't aware the business was being sold. The suggested solution was that she would be prepared to spend a few days with us after the sale had completed, as long as she was compensated with a full time rate of pay. This didn't seem a very satisfactory way to proceed. Financially it wouldn't make a lot of difference (although we definitely thought that it was taking the piss), but this unhelpful attitude just made us on edge about the overall situation.

After several weeks of trying we finally managed to agree that a face to face meeting on site would be the best way to get to the bottom of the remaining issues and hopefully set a timescale for completion.

The first thing we asked was to look at the stock, the majority of which was stored in the basement. It transpired that the bulk of the £10,000 value was attributed to boxes and boxes of large vases of various styles, which were allegedly in constant use for weddings and other events. In our eyes these didn't look to be something that would be in great demand and literally seemed to just be collecting dust. There really didn't seem to be much more to the stock than that, other than a couple of ornamental display stands that might be used on the odd occasion, leaving us back at our original mindset that we didn't want to take on this part of the deal.

While discussing the general running of the business and trying to get some sense around a handover, it was mentioned that the main part time florist had given notice to leave. This was presented to us as a positive development as it would reduce the wage bill, but taking into account the lack of support being offered during the transition period, this was probably the biggest knock to our confidence in carrying on.

And a final push in the wrong direction was that the one remaining member of staff had now found out that the shop was for sale and was apparently interested in making an offer herself.

We talked about all these concerns when we got back home, our worry was that we could press ahead and take over the shop, only to find that we would be handed the keys without knowing so much as where the light switches were, no longer having the well regarded staff member to assist and left with one disgruntled part timer to boot.

After much soul searching and weighing up all the points we came to the crushing conclusion that there would be too many risks involved to carry on, so we instructed our solicitors to withdraw the offer.

Drawing a line under this whole episode in September 2019, it was actually quite hard for us both to come to terms with as we had looked at it as a way to take control of our own destiny and lay the foundations for a positive new beginning.

Now it felt like we were right back at square one, with no outlet for Taylor to put her floristry skills into practice and no prospect of a rational way for me to escape my work situation.

My motivation levels were at an all time low for tackling 9 hours sitting in a windowless office full of stress, sandwiched between a horrible daily commute. It didn't take too long for us to decide we needed to do something to force a detour to the route our lives were taking; it simply wouldn't be healthy to keep trudging along regardless.

Chapter Fourteen

2020 to 2021
Age - 44 to 45

So after talking through several ideas, we decided to take a year off work, well more like quit.
In hindsight I'm sure I could have negotiated some kind of sabbatical time off, giving me a wage to return to, but I feel that may have diluted the feeling of it being a fresh start.
Our plan was to buy a camper van, do some test trips, making them gradually longer and longer, then go away for at least six months.

After many weeks of searching and viewing different vans, we found exactly what we were looking for. It's a bit of a unique set-up, having two bench seats at the back which turn into a double bed and a separate seat near the front which also turned into a single bed and could have its own table as well.
We had to travel nearly 250 miles each way to view it and then again to pick her up.
The previous owners referred to the van as Betsy, and as we had passed through the awesomely named Betws-y-Coed (pronounced Betsy co ed) on the way, the name stuck.
With this piece of the jigsaw slipping into place nicely, the time came to make a bold decision on the work

front. After looking through our finances carefully we figured out that we could comfortably take the whole of 2020 off and afford to spend at least 9 months travelling around having fun.

I was consciously trying to force myself into a situation to decide what career or way of life I wanted for the remainder of my working years.

One of the most clichéd of clichés must be to take a gap year travelling in order to "find yourself", but for myself and Taylor it was intended to be just that. The metaphorical pressing of the Reset button and literal break in employment would inevitably result in large scale changes to our lives by the time this sabbatical came to an end.

I had no idea what I wanted to pursue at this stage and was open to any possibility as long as it ended up being something that I enjoy and can become competent at.

I made certain to leave my existing job on very good terms, providing a last resort Plan B of returning to the company I kind of despised if all else failed.

My department had grown by now and I had a deputy to help with a lot of the admin of the job, so I informed him that I might be putting my notice in to finish by the end of the year. He was interested in moving up to the manager position which I said I'd pass on.

I arranged a meeting with the CEO and told him I was going to quit, giving just over a months notice. I explained small parts of the background and made it clear that some of the reason was due to a lack of support, alluding to his own failings and instances where he had sabotaged my progress. It was a friendly conversation and before leaving I said "There's a chance I'll be knocking on your door in 12 months."

With this leap made, our thoughts turned to planning our mini adventures.
We used our new home on wheels to great effect when visiting relatives over Christmas, which gave us the chance to practice our vanlife skills while also mapping out some trips in the New Year.
We had one early test run on Morecambe seafront, which was bitterly cold in the morning and not very comfortable as we hadn't figured out how to turn the heating on. But we had a nice night and sketched out some short circular routes that we planned to do as soon as possible.
When we moved on to look at actually booking campsites, it quickly became clear that most of them didn't open until the end of March, something we hadn't considered.
This wouldn't stop us, as the van was set up for off-grid use, but we decided to wait a couple of months before tackling any longer trips.
Around this same time, at the beginning of January 2020, major developments were happening globally with the emergence of the (spoiler alert, if you've not heard about it!) Coronavirus / Covid-19 "pandemic".
I have a lot of opinions on this entire subject, which I may write about elsewhere, but in summary I feel that the wrong approach has been taken completely and any serious threat could have been dealt with by providing correct treatments for the small demographic of people

that are at serious risk. I have massive issues with the "mandated" use of masks, lockdowns and vaccines for entire populations.

The first lockdown was coincidentally just as we were hoping to get started on our vanlife tours. The uncertainty of whether we could travel without being questioned by the police stopped us leaving the house for a number of weeks. Even if we did try to go away, it was impossible to plan ahead as events were being cancelled, or tourist attractions closed. We'd been gifted a year's membership for the National Trust but the majority of sites were closed or only partially open.

Time dragged on and we settled into a bit of a lazy lifestyle, although I still kept busy working in the garden and doing bits of DIY. Tay encouraged me to just enjoy some downtime as it's the only time in life it's likely to be this way. But my restless personality meant I was always either finding things to do, or spending most of the time fretting that I wasn't getting enough done. I tried tackling this by revisiting some of the mindfulness techniques from the low level counselling I'd had. This did help and it gave me the opportunity to reflect on my life.
As this progressed I had the urge to start writing again.
Even more of a cliché, taking a sabbatical to write "one's Book"!

Initially I slipped back into my persistent problem of trying to write about a distinct subject while crowbarring in my back story in wherever possible. But as the circumstances presented themselves I grasped the nettle and decided I would have a go at writing some form of Autobiography or Memoir. Both of those heavily laden terms feel uncomfortable to me, given the fierce aversion I have to attracting any attention, so I just call it "my book".
And even that sounds wanky, but so be it.

So from trusting just one person on the planet with the inescapable baggage I carry, I've decided now to document it for absolutely anyone on the planet to be able to read. Well, if you read English at least.
Is that even a good idea? I suppose it's the only way that I can manifest a sense of closure for myself, other than taking my abuser to court.
I feel that I'm past that now though, I don't need to go through the (no doubt shitty) process and uncertainty that any prosecution involves. At the time the abuse was happening, I wouldn't do anything like that to avoid my dark secret being public, but now I just don't care.

Even after writing quite a large chunk of the content, my conviction to complete it and publish still wavered and without the next development I believe my ideas would have fizzled out once more, with a 75% finished manuscript languishing here on my laptop.

That event, that has definitely changed the path of my life from that point on. That might sound hyperbolic, for such a seemingly insignificant event as "watching the sunrise", but it gave me the framework to build a home for a lot of the weird and wonderful ideas that rattle through my brain.

On Saturday May 16th, the National Trust ran a live event called Dawns Live. I think I covered most aspects of the idea in the Introduction, so to recap it resulted in the concept of marking the start of each month by taking the time out to spend from Dark through until Light. The culmination of these visits is clearly the actual point of Sunrise itself, but the process leading up to that is of much greater importance.

For myself, as the idea has developed, it has transitioned into not just the literal observance of the arrival of daytime, but each rendition acting as its own mental re-evaluation of your life at identifiable, regular points in time and how that relates to the overall timeline of the years ahead of you. (487 months at time of writing....oooh just over 40 years, I can live with that!)

There is also the potential to turn this ether-like concept into a physical, viable community, which is something I'm working on in the background. Most likely these ideas will fizzle out and come to nothing, but I'd love to create a website as a home for my random acts of Content.

As I see it I could publish my book there and set up a Patreon type account where I would upload the "living book" section of this project - Volume Two - 500 Sunsets Remaining, aiming to update it on a monthly basis.

There could be a Dark to Light club, where people join my cult, oops I mean religion, getting as many people as possible to follow a similar ritual within their own schedule.

I'd love to hear people's stories and see the photos from other parts of the world; I feel that it would be a great community to engage with in these shitty Big Tech social media times.

There are many more crazy schemes up my sleeve that would mesh nicely with my overall feel for the website, so hopefully I can stop procrastinating and get on and do it. Maybe tomorrow…..

Anyway, back to the book. I began by writing the Introduction, kind of obvious I guess, but it also served as a way for me to visualise what I was trying to achieve.

I said at the end of the Intro, "Now comes the hard part" and that sentiment rang true as I tapped away trying to piece together a Chronology of my life. I had never approached the subject of my history in this way before, definitely not in black and white, but even in my head I have only looked at individual periods and events.

Quite soon after I started I must have unlocked a number of previously forgotten memories. My fingers had a hard time keeping up with my brain as I skipped down the page to add various reminder notes and phrases in random years. Thoughts that I feared would drift away again given half a chance. The technique worked and I maintained the motivation to keep going back and doing the hard slog of stringing all these parts together into a comprehensible "storyline".

I'm still not content with my writing style, as I battle to invoke any emotion through my words, feeling awkward about using overly expressive language to convey my feelings.

But recently, as a side project me and Tay have been doing some creative writing which has helped a lot as I progress and when I go back to make more revisions. She really is a fantastic creative writer and I've learnt a lot from her. I love the little letters we send to each other, which in time may even form part of an idea for the website and would lay the foundations for another interesting community of likeminded people.

Another key moment that created a significant fork in the trajectory of my life happened within just days of the Dawns Live event. I had broken the lockdown "laws" in order to pay a visit to my oldest brother in the middle of May 2020. I've been making efforts to keep in touch with him more and to meet up when possible and on this occasion we went round to his daughters house for a barbecue.

I was aware that I had a great-nephew and had seen him a few times when he was a baby, but I hadn't factored in that Lennon (not his real name) was now nearly six years old and had a massive character and personality of his own.

While watching him have a mini water fight with his mum and his grandad and the unadulterated joy in Lennon's innocent reactions, seeing how it allowed my brother to really let his guard down and just be happy in the moment.

And something else I'm usually uncomfortable seeing, love. It was just obvious how much love there was between them and I was a bit jealous that I can't be that expressive.

Then something unusual happened, a child appeared to like me. I'm usually so standoffish that kids just move on to someone they can get more of a reaction from. Lennon has so much energy and never stops harassing you, pushing to see how much he can get away with, eventually resorting to hitting you with a nerf gun. But I think by being firm and giving him a clear boundary, he gravitated toward me as an authority figure. Now, I am not used to that at all, totally the opposite.

And it felt weird.

So he was pointing nerf guns in my face and running around, having fun and I don't normally join in, or I try to limit my involvement to avoid embarrassment later on.

But I did join in for once, and it felt fun, I enjoyed just messing about. I am too reserved and worried about losing my inhibitions normally to be overtly happy, but kids really don't care or have a filter, which forces you to play along, or look like a total dick.

I have done the latter many times. But this time I actually tried to have fun which was easy as Lennon is very lively. Maybe because they are the only family that I am in contact with of this type, all of a sudden I felt like I wanted to make more of an effort to see them more.

After a few hours of the high energy level, with no sign of it stopping, you do have to wonder how hard it is if it's like that every day. But I've become more receptive to the idea that the potentially short term upsides in having a kid, could outweigh the longer term challenging times.

It did feel like I'd made a new friend. And I never do that, again not for lack of trying (although I haven't tried as hard as I could I guess), but it very rarely happens, to the extent that I joke about wanting a T-Shirt that says "I can't even make online friends".

Time for another musical interlude here, as this foul-mouthed, creepy, awesome video does a better job than I can at relaying how much of an outsider I've always felt in life.

I am a alien
No matter how hard I try I don't fit in
Always all on my own, sad and lonely

All I want is for someone to play with me
I close my eyes and float into the night I like to let my mind drift
Make a jump into a new dimension
Thank God I got that gift

https://youtu.be/yF2y5y7BxgM

Granted, Lennon was only 5 years old and probably likes every new person he meets, but I thought, you know what, fuck it, I'll just have to produce my own friend.
If only there was a way to grow them in a pod until they were about 4 or 5, then pop out when they're nearly ready for fun times!

It's hard to overstate how big a sea change this was in my outlook on life. Up to the age of 44 years old I can truthfully say that my conscious, reasoned decision to never have children was set in stone. For my own personal reasons but as the years go by, also due to the crumbling nature of the freedoms that we should be allowed to live by.
And the ever present fact that I know I would be overly protective to the point where it could potentially create an unhealthy environment. In my usual fashion, I couldn't just approach this subject in a normal manner, instead concocting a grand scheme whereby we would call our baby Truman (yes, even if it was a girl!) and

develop some kind of subscription-only reality TV show charting the life of a human being from a bump all the way through childhood and who knows, a complete lifetime.

To "sell" this idea to my wife, I used my newfound video editing skills and created a very funny (in my opinion) short film where I laid out the proposition. The decision to be made at the end -

Have a baby, call it Truman and start gathering content, or do the sensible thing and never bring a child into this nonsensical "civilisation" that we find ourselves in.

After many long conversations we decided to give it a whole-hearted attempt for the next 6 months or so, then re-evaluate if Tay didn't fall pregnant.

Despite tracking a fertility timer and other measures like cutting down drinking and eating healthier, by November there was still no sign of anything happening.

During this period the world around us only seemed to become more unsettling, with extended lockdowns and ridiculous mask mandates being the most visible upshot. I've been following various global events closely since around 2015 and there are many deeply concerning developments building that only increased my worries about our future freedoms.

Although she never became pregnant, there was one episode in October where Tay had some unusual pains which she put down to being implantation bleeding . This slightly upsetting case seemed to put her off continuing to try, maybe being concerned that at 38 she had missed the opportunity to have children without IVF or other treatments. So we had a casual chat about it and it was left that we wouldn't actively try but for the next few months, not be too careful and if it happens it happens. The overriding feeling was that we'd been right all along and were content with our original stance to never have kids.

This did strike a bit of a blow to my writing, as I could see that it would be a very interesting perspective to document as I continue my memoirs with live updates. For some reason I couldn't generate the motivation to keep trawling through my tangled history trying to put it into a readable format. All my efforts just became another document saved on my laptop that I'd no doubt soon forget I'd even started, until stumbling across it in a few years time.

I even slacked off with my Dark to Light walks, treating a random mid-October outing as my entry for the 1st of November, as I couldn't be bothered to go. And when I missed the 1st of December pilgrimage I totally forgot until nearly the end of the month.

As the end of the year approached, the time had come to consider getting back into some kind of work. The enforced inactivity during our supposed gap year meant that there was no eureka moment where I'd discovered what I wanted to do with my life. The thoughts of crawling back to my previous employer were unpleasant, but it may come to that. The only outlet I'd had was a short stint for an exciting new start-up in the industry I've got 20 years experience. They employed me as a consultant but I could immediately tell that it would go nowhere. Things went quiet after only a couple of months and this work dried up, so I decided to allow myself until the end of January without even considering getting a job. This meant we could have an enjoyable, chilled festive period, before admitting defeat and edging back into the monotony of "normal" life.

And then it happened. The thing that would ultimately change my life forever, whether I liked it or not. As I tinkered in the garage on a lazy Boxing Day morning, Tay sent me a Whatsapp message that simply said "I'm pregnant"
I was 95% sure she was just winding me up so my immediate reply was the Ant and Dec GIF - "Psyche!" I made my way to the bathroom to find my wife sitting on the floor with two different pregnancy tests showing Positive and a third one that she was too scared to look at. Obviously that also came up positive and I exited stage left with a parting shot of "It's a Christmas Miracle!"

Predictably this news immediately rekindled my thoughts of writing and the very next morning I woke up at about 4am, my mind racing and decided to go for a walk, which I now class as my Dark to Light entry for the start of December. On arriving home I picked up where I had left off with my book and settled back into writing a good number of words each session.

My feelings when trying to come to terms with impending Fatherhood were confusing, having recently accepted that it was not a path I'd vigorously choose to follow. But quite quickly I came to realise that I would have felt some regret at not procreating, as my own life finally begins to become a more complete and positive experience. If anything, it is a natural instinct to want to mate and one that I had denied myself venomously for so many years. So I faced up to the challenge and tried to look forward to all the amazing good times that this can bring, while putting in place plans to ensure we can live our lives in the manner we desire and mitigate any negative impact this crazy world might throw at us.

I discovered a couple of amazingly appropriate songs during this period of time, one that sums up my growing desire to conquer my demons and live life to the full - Pop Evil - Waking Lions. The other (that appears at the very end of this book) is a barracking reminder for me to follow through with my intentions, if I really want it.

https://youtu.be/DOhsP6F2RmQ

Is this better, tell me that's a better way
I'm not afraid, I'm not gonna hide from the
Vultures above, serpents below
They wanna lay me to rest, but I won't go
Yeah
Is it better to die than live another day
I'm not afraid, I'm not gonna run from the

Scars held within, burning the skin
They wanna lay me to rest, but I won't go
Yeah
I won't go
I wanna stand up, a hundred feet tall
Cause fear will never lead my way
I'm ready to run, a hundred miles strong
I will never be the same

Waking the lions in me
I'm waking the lions in me

Inevitably the convoluted "Truman Show" element of the whole baby endeavour hasn't quite panned out. Yet another victim of the Structure of Crazy Ideas. Although, the concept is not completely dead, as I have ideas of other ways to document what I see as being a particularly interesting time in domestic and global politics; using the platform of my personal circumstances as a way to commentate on what I perceive to be a Fourth Generational Warfare situation.

The only way I can tackle the upcoming challenges is to take control of our lifestyle to create a little bubble of our own and become external observers of the surrounding chaos. This will primarily involve schooling our child from home, as I see the public school system as more an indoctrination than education. My priority of having a job that I enjoy has now morphed into being something I can tolerate, preferably able to work from home and within my own time schedule.

I think this is the perfect point to conclude Volume One, with my mind made up that I want to publish this Memoir and share it with close family and friends as a minimum. The decision to make it more publicly available is a big one, but I feel like it could be a net positive overall.
Since taking part in the Dawns Live event, my life has changed dramatically and although not everything is perfect, it has metaphorically been a journey from Dark to Light.

Volume Two

December 2020
494 Sunsets Remaining

Having lost all motivation for my Dark to Light outings, I nearly skipped December completely (Sacrilege!) until our big news on the 27th. Such a life changing event as becoming a dad clearly needed some space to come to contemplate. I managed to squeeze in a walk to Heron Island, setting off about 730am on the 30th. Despite the not uncommon lack of an actual sunrise, I managed to snap a few great pictures of a factory across the river, with its blue lights reflecting spooky branches like they were reaching out to you. This time for reflection worked its usual magic and allowed me to put things into perspective. Were all the jigsaw pieces finally clicking into place?
The prospect of bringing up a child creates limitless subjects to write about, if only for my own mental processing. It has inspired me to finally get my book printed if nothing else.
As I sat on the quaint bridge I pondered many difficult issues like schooling, vaccinations, internet and social media, knowing the damage each of those can cause, handled badly. But the overriding feeling is that this is it, my life can finally begin to change for the better.
I made a conscious decision to make this the fresh start I'd always wanted. Whatever happens from now on, I'm going to try to enjoy my life more and have confidence in my convictions.

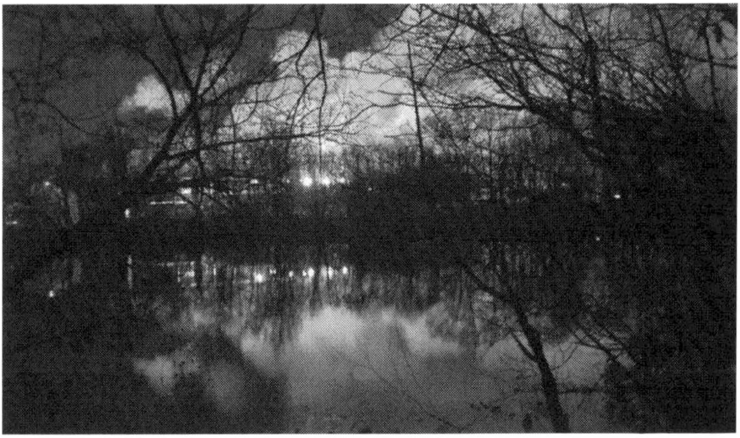

January 2021
493 Sunsets Remaining

Having planned a New Years Eve online quiz, (standard fayre in the "new-normal"), I planned my January Dark to Light for the 2nd. Taylor didn't want anyone to know she was pregnant for another few weeks, so she had sparkling grape juice in a flute as a prop. We had a fun evening and it topped off one of the best Christmas periods that I can remember.
Heading out at 730am on the 2nd, I decided to walk across a nearby golf course, as there looked to be a decent hill with views of the city to the East.
As I tested out the best looking vistas, I saw a deer scampering across the fairway and through two fields. I love seeing wild deer, it still amazes me that they exist in this country. It's nice seeing them in a deer park, but somehow doesn't compare to unexpected encounters.
Only a couple of notable dates for this month, Carls 46th birthday, actually on that day, and my paternal grandads deathday on the 22nd, who died in 2005. Wow, time really is a freakish thing. If I'd been asked how long ago he passed away, I could have easily been wrong by at least 5 years, either side.
Not much else to report, having completed Decembers entry only a couple of days ago.

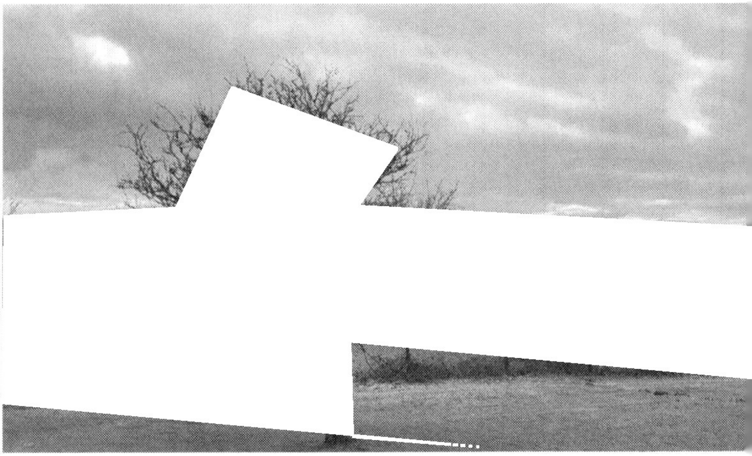

February 2021
492 Sunsets Remaining

Making use of Betsy, I set off at 530am and drove to the top entrance of Williamson Park, with a flask of coffee and various snacks. I parked up and assessed the horrendous blizzard that had swept in. I aimlessly walked around, covering 4 miles in all, investigating different paths as I went; eventually discovering a small lake with a nice bridge that led up to a pagoda-like structure. This appeared to be the optimum spot for a clear view to the East. Clear, other than for the dense cloud and snow.

Time to sit down with my coffee and check this month's notes, which include the three year anniversary of my uncle Teds Deathday. I have started to retain more information in my short term memory in the last couple of years, maybe a sign that I have made some progress as my life has straightened out.

It still came as a shock that three years had passed, but I have clear memories of the funeral which was genuinely funny, with one anecdote literally calling him a wanker from the church podium.

I thought ahead to next month and planned to meet up with Adam as it would be his birthday on the 24th. This potential visit to my old home town started more cogs churning, as I considered driving around, doing a little reminiscing before going to his flat.

March 2021
491 Sunsets Remaining

I've had this location in mind for a Dark to Light mission for a while now, having seen Warton Quarry nearby on a previous outing. I'd figured out a good spot to park, leaving a 1 mile walk through dense woods in near pitch darkness. I was hoping this would bring me to a perfect vantage point looking out across the quarry and towards the mountains in the background.

The torchlight trek was eerie, being in near silence, punctuated by a free shot of adrenaline when some kind of grouse exploded into flight as I stood on a twig. I like these interruptions, it makes the trip more interesting.

Plenty of time to mull over the month ahead, as I set off at 430am, with a 7am Sunrise to get in position for. Along with my brothers birthday, it would have been Tays dads 65th birthday. It's a cruel shame that he'd never know that he would actually become a grandad, despite that prospect being a farfetched reality all the years he was alive.

Tays 12 week scan was in the middle of February, after which we'd started telling family and close friends. This certainly made everything seem a lot more real.

I'd already sorted dates for my visit to Southport, planning a mini vanlife trip and maybe a bonus Dark to Light.

Running through where I was up to with my writing, I came to the conclusion that now would be a good time to contact Sean on Facebook with my intention to arrange a meet up and chat about old times.

As 7am approached I was greeted with an alien looking pink and orange skyline, mists hanging over the distant mountains and a small bright disc for a few minutes. A rare and welcome sight, to see the actual sun rise for once. I even managed to wedge my phone into some branches and set a self timer for a couple of nice photos of me sat on the cliff edge, looking thoughtful!

April 2021
490 Sunsets Remaining

As I set off cycling along the canal at 450am, I had plenty to contemplate. A few days earlier I had visited Southport, with the familiar drive sparking lots of memories from that most painful time of my life. I passed the stables where I'd spent a couple of years full of social awkwardness and the occasional moment of happiness, followed by two sights of my abusers' former workplaces and a small diversion to remind myself what the brass band practice hall looked like. I wondered if the band was still going and quickly found their website and noted that some of the main characters were still involved. Interesting line of inquiry at some point maybe.

I met Adam and had a takeaway for tea, then made my way to Sean's house which felt very surreal given that the last time I saw him was 30 years previous.

After briefly meeting his wife and 3 basically adult kids, we headed for the amazing man shed that he'd built at the bottom of the garden. As we chatted I was able to piece together a much stronger understanding of the timeline and details from our couple of years as best friends. I tried to let him do most of the talking, wondering if the subject of Peter would come up and if there were ever any suspicions. Two hours passed in what felt like 5 minutes and as I could tell Sean was needed in the house, I realised I'd have to cut to the chase. I directed the conversation to the gym and probed his memory of the family and more specifically Peter.

I asked if he remembered the "spitting" incident, which I don't think he did, but it brought back the time he was being picked up to go training. After his description matched many of my examples I explained how that behaviour led to him grooming and abusing me.

His reaction was complete shock, which at least gave me the comforting knowledge that *he* hadn't been abused. He was very supportive and talking about it lifted a heavy burden from my shoulders. I decided to let them get back to their evening and I'd come back the following week for another chat.

It was good to be able to run through it again without rushing and hear more about the various jobs he'd had all over the world. After hearing my story and thoughts about getting closure, Sean's absolute conviction that I should "Prosecute the cunt", was still a step too far for me to consider. I explained that I was writing an autobiography and intended that to be my way to draw a line under the whole affair. But as I thought about all this, while riding to my Dark to Light destination, I decided that I'd look into the process of reporting something like this and talk it through with Tay before making any contact. If anything, it would be good content for Volume Two, right!

I think I've found my favourite new sunrise spot, Glasson View. Not only was there a fantastic view across the River Lune, graced by massive flocks of geese heading South, but a cute looking church whose graveyard looked out over the bay. As the fabled time of sunrise arrived I was treated to another fine display, the rocks showing through the shallow water, creating a stark contrast to the willowy peach and blue skies.

Adam came to stay for a few days, helping me to dig out a corner of the garden that had been used as a dumping ground for the previous owners. During this time I tried to jog his memory to see if he would ask anything about Peter, but he didn't take the bait. I figured that at worst I would just give him the completed version of this book and uncover my past this way.

I talked things over with Taylor and did some research on the process, then contacted NAPAC again for some reassurance. They are unable to offer legal advice so we just talked it through and it became clearer what decisions I would have to make. The conclusion I reached was that in the month that marked my 45th year on this cursed planet, I would inform the police of the abuse I'd suffered over 30 years ago. And I will be writing the second Volume of this book in near Live monthly updates, chronicling this legal process, while also coming to terms with becoming a dad in the next few months, having no job and a leaky campervan that we would have to look at swapping for a safe family car. Add to this the creeping authoritarianism affecting our lives in very real ways and I think it should be interesting to document the next 40 or so years, or more to the point, the 489 Sunsets Remaining.

Nothing More - Do you really want it?

https://youtu.be/T3E6AKDbI2Y

Everybody wants to change the world
But one thing's clear
No one ever wants to change themselves
That's the way things are
All because we hate the buzzkill
Jaded when we need to feel
But we can change it all
If you really want it

Do you really want it?

Thanks to….

Firstly, thanks to my wife who's loving relationship and support finally allowed me to break my curse.

Anyone who has known me, sorry if I've been a dick sometimes, but I hope I've portrayed some mitigating circumstances that will allow me a bit of leeway!

Got to give Dawns Live a mention, as this one off event motivated me to get up at stupid o'clock once a month and gave me the time to sit and think about life, I don't think I would have wrote this book if I hadn't started my "Dark to Light" pilgrimage.

References

A brilliant book to read for anyone that has suffered childhood abuse is Breaking Free - https://www.amazon.co.uk/Breaking-Free-survivors-sexual-Insight/dp/0859698106

NAPAC - National Association for People Abused in Childhood - https://napac.org.uk/

If you suffer from Misophonia, check out Allergic to Sound and Facebook support groups - they've really helped me to cope with this condition.

www.allergictosound.com

https://www.facebook.com/groups/misophoniasupport

I really hope the National Trust team set up another Dawns Live event, keep an eye on their website for any updates - https://www.dawns.live/

Printed in Great Britain
by Amazon